Air University

Style and Author Guide

April 2005

—————————— Air University Press ——————————
Maxwell Air Force Base, Alabama

First Printing April 2005
Second Printing May 2006
Third Printing September 2006

Air University Press
131 West Shumacher Avenue
Maxwell AFB AL 36112-6615

Published by Books Express Publishing
Copyright © Books Express, 2011
ISBN 978-1-78039-974-4

Books Express publications are available from all good retail and online booksellers. For
publishing proposals and direct ordering please contact us at: info@books-express.com

Contents

Foreword

The faculty, staff, and students of Air University—longtime, productive members of the academic community—will find that AU-1, *Air University Style and Author Guide* is designed to unify their writing stylistically and to give them information about publishing with AU Press. Rapid expansion in the field of electronic media—especially the Internet—has made AU research and writing increasingly accessible. For that reason, we should assure that our efforts in these areas are sound—not only substantively but also stylistically. Based on recognized but forward-looking principles of standard English usage, the *Air University Style Guide for Writers and Editors*, part one of this publication, provides reliable guidance on such matters as punctuation, capitalization, abbreviation, documentation, numbers, spelling, and much more. Following the advice found there will make AU publications stylistically consistent and acceptable. Part two, the *Air University Press Author Guide*, contains instructions to writers who wish to have their studies considered for publication by the Air Force's air and space power publisher. I commend AU-1 to your use.

JOHN F. REGNI
Lieutenant General, USAF
Commander, Air University

Preface

I take great pleasure in introducing this new edition of AU-1, *Air University Style and Author Guide*. Officially serving as AU's arbiter of style since 2001, the *Air University Style Guide for Writers and Editors*, part one of this publication, has assisted many writers who have labored in the composition trenches. It offered guidance unofficially for many years before that when it served as the in-house stylebook for Air University Press. The *Style Guide* provides guidance to Air University's community of writers, whether students preparing papers or theses for an AU school or college; faculty members developing articles, monographs, or books for publication; or those brave individuals who edit the prose of their students, colleagues, or customers. Writers outside AU who submit material for university-sponsored publications should also find the *Style Guide* useful. Indeed, anyone who has ever wondered whether *airpower* is one word or two, whether *National Command Authorities* is still current, whether *Jr.* is set off by commas, or whether *53* is written with numerals or spelled out will find help in the following pages.

The *Style Guide* doesn't presume to teach its readers *how* to write or edit, but it does offer a coherent, consistent stylistic base for writing and editing. It includes guidance on a number of questions that inevitably arise during the process of composition, basing that guidance not only on the conventional wisdom available in a variety of authoritative sourcebooks, but also on users' specific needs that have emerged since its inception as the *Air University Press Style Guide for Writers and Editors*. By freeing its users from juggling one handbook against another, the guide brings some stylistic consistency to AU writing.

This printing of the *Style Guide* reflects a major reorganization of its entries, with an eye toward making them both more accessible and more transparent in terms of their function. That is, rather than appearing in a straight alphabetical list, dictionary style, as in previous versions, the items in this edition fall into major categories designated *Terms and Usage, Abbreviations, Grammar and Punctuation, Mechanics,* and *Documentation.* The *Mechanics* section is further divided into the component parts *Capitalization, Spelling and Word Formation, Numbers, Italics,* and *Display Dots.* Entries in each section are arranged alphabetically. Other innovations, designed to help locate information quickly and make the *Style Guide* easier to use, include assigning each item a unique number based upon its categorization (e.g., 1.56, 4.2.95), as well as providing a comprehensive index and extensive cross-references.

The *Style Guide* by no means covers every problem that faces writers and editors. For additional help, we recommend *The Chicago Manual of Style*, 15th edition, on which much of this guide relies for stylistic principles. Explanations and/or examples taken from the 15th edition with little or no modification are italicized and followed by the appropriate reference in parentheses (e.g.,

Chicago, 16.3). For spellings and definitions, the *Style Guide* uses *Webster's Third New International Dictionary of the English Language, Unabridged*, and its chief abridgement, *Merriam-Webster's Collegiate Dictionary*, 11th edition (in the guide, the term *dictionary* refers to either or both of these sources). For advice on grammatical issues, we recommend the eighth edition of *Index to English* by Wilma R. and David R. Ebbitt.

Karl Kraus, Austrian satirist, critic, poet, and curmudgeon-at-large, once quipped, "I have decided many a stylistic problem first by head, then by heads or tails." If a harried writer or editor, unsure of where to place that errant comma, reaches for the *Style Guide* rather than leave such a momentous decision to chance, then it will have served its purpose.

For the first time, AU-1 includes between its covers a thoroughly revised edition of the *Air University Press Author Guide*, part two of this publication. As the publishing arm of Air University, the press makes available a number of publications on airpower and space power topics in a variety of formats. The *Author Guide* offers simple, concise instructions both to writers who wish to submit a manuscript to the press for consideration and to individuals whose work has been accepted for publication and who now wish to submit their final package of materials. Since the press uses the *Style Guide* as its in-house manual of style, it makes perfect sense to combine these two resources. Authors can now find answers to stylistic questions that arise during the composition of their manuscripts and learn how to submit their work for publication by consulting one convenient reference. It is our hope that AU-1's new look is to your liking and that you find answers to your questions even more easily than before.

As always, we are indebted to all of the people who reviewed the manuscript and gave their thoughtful suggestions for its improvement. We invite interested writers and editors to send their comments and suggestions for later editions to Dr. Marvin Bassett, the editor of the *Air University Style and Author Guide*. He can be reached at Air University Press, 131 West Shumacher Avenue, Maxwell AFB, Alabama 36112-6615 or by e-mail at aupress.style@maxwell.af.mil.

Dr. Shirley B. Laseter
Director
Air University Library & Press

Part 1

Air University Style Guide for Writers and Editors

1.0 Terms and Usage

This section contains explanations of the conventional use of selected common words (e.g., *a* or *an*, *bimonthly*, *entitle* or *title*, *while*) and of terms having distinctive meanings in publishing (e.g., *caption/legend*, *foreword*, *glossary*, *illustrations/figures*, *running heads*, *tables*). It also provides guidance on the use of terms that might prove distracting or offensive to readers (e.g., *Negro*, *profanity*, *sexist language*) and identifies acceptable variants of certain words (e.g., *US Air Force/Air Force/USAF*, *weapon system/weapons system*, *World War I/World War 1/First World War/Great War*).

1.1　**a/an**. Use *a* before *consonant sounds* and *an* before *vowel sounds*: *a* historical event, not *an* historical event. Since an acronym is usually read as a series of letters or as a word, choose the indefinite article in accordance with the pronunciation of the first letter (*an* NCA decision) or the pronunciation of the word (*a* NATO meeting).

1.2　**above**. You may use *above* to refer to information higher on the same page or on a preceding page:

> There are flaws in the above interpretation.

1.3　**aerospace**. See air and space (1.7).

1.4　**aircraft**. Show model designations by adding the letter without a space: F-4C, B-52H.

1.5　**air force**. Spell out *air force* either as a noun or an adjective. When referring to the *United States Air Force*, you may use that term as well as *US Air Force*, *Air Force*, or *USAF*.

1.6　**Air Force–wide** (adj., adv.). Use an en dash in this compound. See also dash (3.2.6).

1.7　**air and space**. Use this term rather than *aerospace*.

1.8　**and/or**. Acceptable, but don't overuse. According to Ebbitt and Ebbitt (see "Bibliography," p. 181), "*and/or* is used primarily in business writing. . . . It is objected to by some readers because *and/or* looks odd and because *and* or *or* alone is often all that's needed. But it's sometimes useful when there are three alternatives—*both* the items mentioned or *either* one of them: inflation and/or depression" (p. 24). See also slash (3.2.17).

1.9　**arms control** (n.)

1.10 **arms-control** (adj.)

1.11 **art, artwork**. See illustrations (1.33).

1.12 **back matter**. Elements following the main text of a book are known as the back matter. In order, they include appendix(es), chronology (if not in front matter), abbreviations (if not in front matter), glossary, bibliography, list of contributors, and index(es). Use Arabic numerals to number the pages of the back matter.

1.13 **below**. You may use *below* to refer to information lower on the same page or on a following page:

> These exercises, discussed below, are important to a unit's training.

1.14 **biannual, biennial**. *Biannual* and *semiannual* mean twice a year; *biennial* means every two years. For clarity, use *twice a year* or *every two years*.

1.15 **bimonthly**. *Bimonthly* can mean every two months or twice a month; *semimonthly* means twice a month. For clarity, use *every two months* or *twice a month*.

1.16 **biweekly**. *Biweekly* can mean every two weeks or twice a week. For clarity, use *every two weeks* or *twice a week*.

1.17 **black (people)** (n., adj.). You may either capitalize or lowercase *black(s)*; choose one style, and use it consistently. See also Negro, Negroes (1.39); white (people) (1.70).

1.18 **caption/legend**. *These terms, sometimes used interchangeably, refer to explanatory material that appears immediately below an illustration (figure, photograph, etc.). Not necessarily a full sentence, the caption/legend can consist of two or more sentences or a title followed by one or more full sentences* (*Chicago*, 12.8). The caption/legend follows the figure number on a line parallel to and flush left with the bottom of the illustration. Place a period at the end if it is a complete sentence; preferably, use sentence-style capitalization even if it is not a complete sentence (see also titles of works [4.1.148]; tables [1.55]). Do not use a period at the end of a caption/legend that is an incomplete sentence unless you follow it with a complete sentence:

> Figure 1. Carrier air wing. As the Air Force assembles composite wings, it would do well to study how the Navy operates its carrier air wings. The composite nature of the carrier air wing is evident from this deck photo of the USS *Theodore Roosevelt* and its complement of aircraft.
>
> Figure 2. System flowchart applied to mission accomplishment

Note that the figure designation and caption/legend may be set in boldface:

Figure 2. Operationally responsive space: view of near-space architecture

Figure 3. Responsiveness of space architecture. The ORS initiative divides improvements in responsiveness into categories that include the space vehicle, launch vehicle, and infrastructure. Improving each of these areas simultaneously presents a challenge. (Reprinted from briefing, Lt Col Gus Hernandez, Headquarters Air Force Space Command [AFSPC], Directorate of Plans and Requirements, subject: ORS Overview, 7 March 2005.)

If the caption/legend is the title of a work of art, use headline-style capitalization and italics (Chicago, 12.33):

Figure 9. *Starry Night*

An illustration number may be separated from the caption/legend by a period or, if the number is typographically distinct, by a space. The word "figure" may be either spelled out or abbreviated as "fig." (Chicago, 12.34):

Fig. 1. US bomb tonnage dropped on Germany by month

Figure 3 US airpower versus the world

Plate 3 Venice in winter

Identify the source of an illustration with a credit line. *Place it at the end of the caption/legend, in parentheses or in different type (or both) (Chicago, 12.42). Use "reprinted from" or "adapted from,"* depending upon whether you have copied the illustration or modified it, respectively:

Figure 3. Competitive effects on general and administrative costs. (Adapted from Maj Paul G. Hough, "Financial Management for the New World Order," *Airpower Journal* 6, no. 3 [Fall 1992]: 51.)

A photographer's name occasionally appears in small type parallel to the bottom side of a photograph (Chicago, 12.42). For material that the author has obtained free and without restrictions, the word "courtesy" may appear in the credit line (Chicago, 12.46):

Photograph courtesy of Col Mike Schrieve

Mayor Lunsford at the groundbreaking ceremony for the industrial plant, September 2002. Courtesy of Cathi Fredericks.

Unless fair use applies (see appendix C), *an illustration reproduced from a published work under copyright requires permission (Chicago, 12.47):*

Reproduced by permission from T. R. Fehrenbach, *This Kind of War* (Washington, DC [or D.C.]: Brassey's, 2000), facing 237.

If you use words such as *left*, *right*, *top*, *bottom*, or *left to right* to identify individual subjects within an illustration, put them in italics, preceding the subjects they identify:

Figure 1. *Left to right*: George Jones, Henry Johnson, and John Hopkins

Figure 3. *Upper left*, B-1; *upper right*, F-15; *lower left*, C-5; *center*, XV-3; *lower right*, XV-15

If your table of contents includes a list of illustrations, do not simply reprint the captions/legends as they appear in the text. If they are lengthy, you should shorten them:

[caption]: The White Garden, reduced to its bare bones in early spring. The box hedges, which are still cut by hand, have to be carefully kept in scale with the small and complex garden as well as in keeping with the plants inside the "boxes."

[entry in list]: The White Garden in early spring (Chicago, 12.55)

See also illustrations/figures (1.33).

1.19 click. One kilometer.

1.20 copyright. See appendix C of this guide.

1.21 dates. Write exact dates in the sequence day-month-year, without commas. Spell out the month, use figures for the day, and use a four-digit year. When you use only the month and year, no commas are necessary:

FDR referred to 7 December 1941 as a day that would live in infamy.

The date March 2003 was special to her.

Do not use the all-numeral style for dates (3/11/50, etc.) in formal writing. However, in text discussing the events of [11 September 2001,] the use of 9/11 is acceptable (Chicago, 6.115). If documentation, figures, and tables contain numerous dates, you may abbreviate certain months (Jan., Feb., Mar., Apr., May, June, July, Aug., Sept., Oct., Nov., Dec.) and use the sequence day-month-year without internal punctuation (7 Dec. 1941) to reduce clutter (Chicago, 9.39, 15.42, 17.225). Choose one style for the documentation, figures, and tables, and use it consistently. See also numbers (4.3).

1.22 direct quotations. See quotations (5.3).

1.23 dot-com (n., adj.). A company that markets its products or services online via a World Wide Web site.

1.24 East Berlin, East Germany. Use *East Berlin or East Germany*, not just *Berlin* or *Germany* alone, in references to the city and country when they were divided.

1.25 **entitle, title** (v.). The terms *entitle* and *title* are used interchangeably in the sense of designating or calling by a title: A book entitled [*or* titled] *Roderick Random* was on the list of required readings.

1.26 **epigraph**. An epigraph is a pertinent quotation that may be used at the head of a chapter. Do not enclose an epigraph in quotation marks. Set it in italics in the same sized type as the text or in Roman a size smaller. *Identify the source of the quotation on the following line. Cite only the author's name (sometimes preceded by a dash) and usually the title of the work. If the author is well known, you may cite the last name only* (*Chicago*, 1.38–.39). Do not place an endnote at the end of an epigraph.

> *A foolish consistency is the hobgoblin of little minds, adored by little statesmen and philosophers and divines.*
>
> —Ralph Waldo Emerson
> *Essays, First Series: Self-Reliance*

1.27 **figures**. See numbers (4.3) or illustrations/figures (1.33), as appropriate.

1.28 **foreword**. A foreword (*not* spelled *forward*) is part of the front matter of a book, appearing before the preface. Usually it is two to four pages long and written by someone other than the author of the book. The name of the person who wrote the foreword appears at the end of the piece. See also front matter (1.29).

1.29 **front matter**. Elements preceding the main text of a book are known as the front matter. In order, they include the title page, copyright page, dedication, epigraph, table of contents, list of illustrations, list of tables, foreword, about the author [AU Press publications], preface, acknowledgments (if not part of preface), introduction (if not part of text), abbreviations (if not part of back matter), and chronology (if not in back matter). Use lowercase Roman numerals to number the pages of the front matter.

1.30 **glossary**. *Include a glossary if you use a number of unfamiliar or technical terms in your text. Arrange the words to be defined in alphabetical order, each word on a separate line and accompanied by its definition. Place the glossary before the bibliography* (*Chicago*, 1.87). See also back matter (1.12).

Glossary of Internet Terms

browser	A client program (software) that is used to look at various kinds of Internet resources.
cookie	The most common meaning of "cookie" on the Internet refers to a piece of information sent by a Web server to a Web browser that the browser software is expected to save and to send back to the server whenever the browser makes additional requests from the server.
download	Transferring data (usually a file) from another computer to the computer you are using. The opposite of *upload*.

If your text includes a number of acronyms or initialisms, you may wish to include them in a list of abbreviations (an umbrella term that includes both acronyms and initialisms), located before the bibliography.

Abbreviations

AWACS	Airborne Warning and Control System
LGB	laser-guided bomb
MANPADS	man-portable air defense system

1.31 **headings**. See subheadings (1.53).

1.32 **idem (the same)**. See notes (5.1).

1.33 **illustrations/figures**. *Illustrations or figures (the terms are pretty much interchangeable) include maps, line drawings, photographs, paintings, or charts (graphs, diagrams, flow charts, bar charts, etc.) (Chicago, 12.3).* Tables are not considered illustrations *even though they may occasionally be listed under a subhead in the list of illustrations (e.g., if space so dictates) (Chicago, 1.47).* See also tables (1.55).

Place an illustration so that it appears as soon as possible after the first text reference to it. It may precede the reference only if it appears on the same page or the same two-page spread as the reference—or if the text is too short to permit placing it after the reference. If a book includes more than a handful of illustrations, they should normally be numbered. However, if the illustrations are neither integral to the text nor specifically referred to, numbers are unnecessary (Chicago, 12.10–.11, 12.15). If appropriate, number illustrations consecutively throughout the text, and refer to them by their numbers, either parenthetically (fig. 8) or as part of the text:

The totals shown in figure 3 are rounded off to the nearest dollar.

Maps are sometimes numbered separately if that is more convenient for readers (Chicago, 12.12).

If each chapter in a book is written by a different author, the numbering of figures and tables restarts with each new chapter. For precise identification of figures and tables, use a combination of chapter number, a period, and figure/table number: 2.1, 2.2., 2.3, and so forth. If a book has appendixes with figures and/or tables, the numbers should include the letter of the particular appendix (A.1, A.2, B.1, B.2, C.1, C.2, etc.).

If illustrations are gathered into a gallery (a section devoted solely to illustrations), they need not be numbered unless referred to in the text. If they are numbered and if other numbered illustrations are interspersed throughout the text, use two number sequences (e.g., "figure

1," etc. for text illustrations and "plate 1," etc. for gallery illustrations) (Chicago, 12.16). It is seldom necessary to list [illustrations printed together in a gallery or galleries] separately in a list of illustrations. Their location may be noted at the end of the table of contents; for example, "Illustrations follow pages 130 and 288" (Chicago, 1.43).

An illustration number may be separated from the caption/legend by a period or, if the number is typographically distinct, by a space. The word "figure" may be either spelled out or abbreviated as "fig." (Chicago, 12.34).

> Fig. 1. US bomb tonnage dropped on Germany by month
>
> Figure 3 US airpower versus the world
>
> **Plate 3** Venice in winter

Identify the source of the illustration with a credit line. Place it at the end of the caption/legend, in parentheses or in different type (or both), introduced by *reprinted from* or *adapted from*, depending upon whether you have copied the illustration or modified it, respectively: Before using an illustration from a copyrighted source, obtain a formal (written) release from the copyright owner. See also caption/legend (1.18); tables (1.55); appendix C.

If a book has either very many or very few illustrations, it is not necessary to include a list of them following the table of contents. Multiauthor books, a collection of symposia proceedings, and so forth do not usually include lists of illustrations. If such a list is included, it may be divided into subheadings if the book contains various types of illustrations (e.g., charts, photographs, plates, drawings, maps, etc.) (Chicago, 1.44–.45).

1.34 **index**. An index helps the reader find details about particular subjects. Meaningful entries direct the reader to pertinent references in the text but not to merely passing remarks. Consult the 15th edition of *The Chicago Manual of Style* (18.1–.149) for information about the preparation of an index.

1.35 **Internet address**. See URL (uniform [or universal] resource locator) (2.425).

1.36 **latitude, longitude**. Spell out the terms *latitude* and *longitude* in text or standing alone: longitude 80 degrees east; the polar latitudes, from 20° 50′ north latitude to 20° 50′ south latitude. In tables you may abbreviate as follows:

> lat 41°15′40″ N
>
> long 90°18′30″ W

1.37   **lists**. Run lists into the text or set them apart in a vertical enumeration. Use Arabic numerals in both styles.

For a run-in enumeration, enclose the numbers in parentheses without a period. Use commas to separate items in a simple series if there is little or no punctuation within the items; otherwise, use semicolons:

> Plain English standards include the following: (1) present material in a logical, orderly sequence, (2) write in a clear, uncluttered style, and (3) write in active voice.

Note that items in the series should be syntactically parallel.

For a vertical enumeration, follow these principles:

1. *Use a grammatically complete sentence (like the one above), followed by a colon, to introduce a vertical list.*

2. *Entries do not require periods at the end unless at least one entry is a complete sentence, in which case each entry requires a period at the end.*

3. *Items in a list should be syntactically similar.*

4. *If items are numbered, as they are in this example, a period follows each number, and each entry begins with a capital letter— whether or not the entry forms a complete sentence.*

5. *Unnumbered items, each of which consists of an incomplete sentence, should begin in lowercase and require no terminal punctuation.*

6. *If a list completes the sentence that introduces it, items begin with lowercase letters; commas or semicolons separate each item; and the last item ends with a period. (Such lists are often better run into the text rather than presented vertically.) (Chicago, 6.127, 6.129).*

Set the list flush with the text or indent. Align run-over lines with the first word after the numeral:

> The following steps increase your effectiveness as a communicator:
>
> 1. Use English that is alive.
> 2. Analyze the purpose and audience, taking care to select a subject that will be of interest to the audience.
> 3. Conduct the research.
> 4. Support your ideas.
>
> Compose three sentences:
>
> 1. To illustrate the use of commas in dates
> 2. To distinguish the use of semicolons from the use of periods
> 3. To illustrate the use of parentheses within dashes

The five categories of research sources are as follows:

abstracts of student papers
Air Force sources
DOD sources
periodicals
other sources

The loan officer told Richard to

1. fill out the application forms,
2. make a copy for himself, and
3. return all paperwork in one week.

1.38 **mottoes**. Enclose mottoes and similar expressions in quotation marks, capitalize them as if they were titles, or capitalize the first word only:

> "A penny saved is a penny earned" was his favorite maxim.
>
> The flag bore the motto Don't Tread on Me.
>
> He was fond of the motto All for one and one for all.

1.39 **Negro, Negroes**. Since the use of *Negro(es)* may sometimes be offensive, use *black(s)* or *Black(s)*, *African-American(s)*, or *Afro-American(s)*. The use of *Negro(es)* is appropriate in certain historical citations: "In October 1940, the War Department announced . . . that Negro Aviation Units would be organized as soon as the necessary personnel were trained." See also white (people) (1.70); black (people) (1.17).

1.40 **nicknames**. Enclose a nickname in quotation marks when it accompanies the full name:

> George Herman "Babe" Ruth

Omit the quotation marks when a nickname is used as part of or in place of a personal name:

> Stonewall Jackson
>
> the Iron Duke

1.41 **percent**. Always spell out *percent* in humanistic text, and precede it with Arabic numerals: a 3 percent increase. You may use the % symbol in tables and in scientific or statistical text.

1.42 **preliminaries**. See front matter (1.29).

1.43 **profanity**. Do not arbitrarily use profanity, vulgarity, abusive/offensive language, and so forth, in any of the writing you do under the auspices of Air University.

1.44 **proofreaders' marks.** The following signs are used in marking manuscripts:

℈	Delete	⊥̸M	Insert em dash
℈	Delete and close up	⊥̸N	Insert en dash
⌒	Close up; delete space	∧;	Insert semicolon
#	Insert space	⊙	Insert colon
¶	Begin new paragraph	⊙	Insert period
□	Indent one em from left or right	(set) ?	Insert question mark
⊏	Move to left	②	Query to author—in margin
⊐	Move to right	(sp)	Spell out
⊐⊏	Center	*tr*	Transpose
⊔	Move down	*wf*	Wrong font—circle letter
⊓	Move up	*bf*	Set in boldface type
∧	Insert marginal addition	*Rom*	Set in roman type
=	Straighten type; align horizontally	*ital*	Set in italic type—underscore word
‖	Align vertically	*cap*	Set in CAPITALS
∧	Insert comma	*s c*	Set in SMALL CAPS
∨	Insert apostrophe (or single quotation mark)	*lc*	Set in lowercase
∨	Insert quotation marks	*C & lc*	Caps and lowercase
∧	subscript (H_2O)	⊥	Lowercase letter
∨	superscript (a^2)	*stet*	Let it stand; restore words crossed out
/=/	Insert hyphen		

NOTE: If you want to underline a word for emphasis, you must so indicate in a marginal note to the printer. All words underscored in a typed manuscript without such a note will always appear in italics.

The following paragraph illustrates the use of proofreaders' marks:

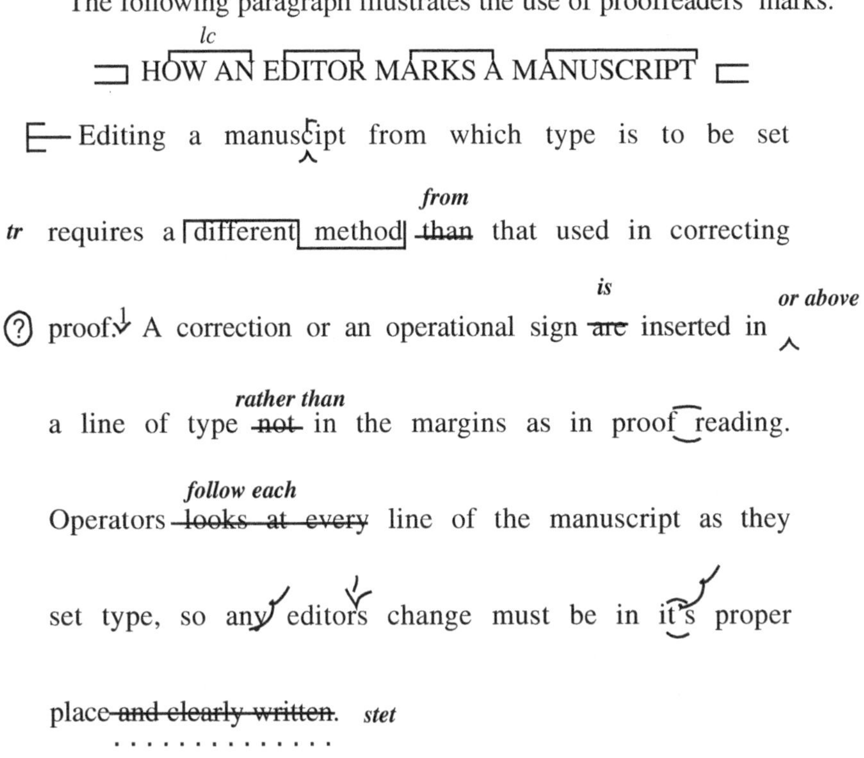

For more information on proofreaders' marks, see the 15th edition of *The Chicago Manual of Style*.

1.45 **retired military personnel**. Use this style in running text: Maj Ronald R. Dowdy, USAF, retired.

1.46 **running heads**. Running heads are located at the tops of pages of published works; they serve as reference points for readers. If running heads are to be included in a book, they should also appear on the pages of the contents, preface, foreword, and so forth (but not on the first page of those parts) when they run more than one page. Use the same running head (e.g., Contents, Preface, etc.) on both the verso (left) and recto (right) pages of these front-matter elements. Headings should not appear on display pages such as the title, disclaimer, dedication, and so forth.

The first page of a chapter should not contain a running head; neither should part titles or any page containing only a table or an illustration. If a page includes both a table (or an illustration) and lines of text, however, it should include a running head. The following are some acceptable arrangements for running heads on text pages (for others, see the 15th edition of the *Chicago Manual of Style*, 1.95):

Verso	*Recto*
Part title	Chapter title
Chapter title	Chapter title
Chapter title	Chapter subtitle
Chapter number	Chapter title
Author (multiauthor books)	Chapter title

Including the book title as a running head on the verso page is no longer common practice since most readers know what book they're reading and would rather have running heads tell them where they are in the book.

Acceptable arrangements for running heads in the back matter include the following:

Verso	*Recto*
Appendix A	Title of appendix
Appendix	Appendix (if not titled)
Glossary	Glossary
Bibliography	Bibliography
Bibliography	Section title
Index	Index

Use running heads on the text pages and those of the front and back matter of any AU Press publication (whether book or monograph) that contains chapters. If a publication does not contain chapters (e.g., a Maxwell Paper or Wright Flyer), do not use running heads on either the text pages or those of the front and back matter. For publications that contain chapters, use running heads in accordance with the guidance above (e.g., if the foreword, preface, etc. run more than one page). Select running heads for the text and front/back matter from the options specified above.

1.47   **Russia, Russian**. Use *Russia* and *Russian* in reference to the nation before 1917; to the former Russian Soviet Socialist Republic; to the independent state formed after the breakup of the Soviet Union in 1991; and to the language and the ethnological origin of the people of that state. See also CIS (Commonwealth of Independent States) (2.92); Soviet(s), Soviet Union, USSR (1.52).

1.48   **semiannual**. Avoid *semiannual*; use *twice a year*.

1.49   **sexist language**. Do not use terms that denigrate or patronize people *(the weaker sex)*, that stereotype occupations by sex (always referring to a nurse as *she* or a pilot as *he*), or that exclude either sex from positions of authority (a *commander* should brief *his* staff on new policy).

You may use pairs of masculine and feminine pronouns *(his or her, he or she, him or her)* in reference to antecedents whose sex is unspecified (every *patient* had *his or her* temperature checked). Such references can become numerous and awkward, however, so use them sparingly. You can avoid this problem by making both the pronoun and antecedent plural (all *patients* had *their* temperatures checked). If the antecedent is an indefinite pronoun *(each, either, neither, one, no one, everyone, someone, anyone, nobody, everybody, somebody, anybody)*, which is considered singular, use a pair of singular pronouns—not a plural pronoun—to refer to it (*everyone* had *his or her* temperature checked [instead of] *everyone* had *their* temperature checked). Avoid the practice of alternating masculine and feminine pronouns in referring to antecedents of unspecified sex (using *she* in one passage and *he* in another) since this may be confusing to readers. Similarly, avoid such clumsy combinations as *he/she* and *s/he* as pronouns of common gender.

You may use *she* (and appropriate variants) in reference to nations, cities, and ships (*Britain* must guard *her* traditions).

You may use *he* (and appropriate variants) in reference to military foes (The *enemy* had massed *his* forces on the border).

You may use *man*, whether freestanding or in compounds, in references to occupations and offices *(policeman, chairman, congressman)* or to both men and women *(mankind, manpower, free men)*. However, if you find such usage offensive or if you believe your audience might, consider substituting gender-neutral terms *(officer, chairperson or chair, member of Congress, persons, people)*.

1.50   **sic (so; thus; in this manner)**. Use *sic*, italicized and bracketed, to indicate misspelling or improper usage in original text:

> The newscaster announced that "the pilot got out of his plane and laid
> [*sic*] down on the ground after his harrowing flight."

1.51   **so-called**. A word or words following *so-called* should not be enclosed in quotation marks or italicized:

> The so-called model citizen beat his wife regularly.

1.52   **Soviet(s), Soviet Union, USSR**. Use *Soviet(s)*, *Soviet Union*, or *USSR* instead of *Russian(s)* or *Russia* in references to the people or the nation from 1917 to 1991. See also CIS (Commonwealth of Independent States) (2.92).

1.53   **subheadings**. Use up to three levels of subheadings to divide text: centered, flush and hang, and run-in (highest to lowest). Text should be divided into at least two parts (i.e., at least two centered, at least two flush-and-hang, and at least two run-in subheadings). If at all possible, do not "stack" headings (i.e., immediately follow one heading with another); rather, separate headings by text. Do not place an endnote at the end of subheadings; instead, find an appropriate place in the running text for the note number.

Observations [centered]

Given this background, the key question remains, Does the
composite wing work in combat? The answer is obvious. . . .

> **Why the Composite Wing Worked So Well [flush and hang]**
> The composite training undergone by the wing's personnel contributed to the successful completion of their mission. . . .
>
> **Evaluation and Inspection**. [run-in] Tactical evaluations, operational readiness inspections, and other exercises have created a solid foundation of training in both units and individuals. . . .

1.54   **subtitle**. Use a colon to separate a title from its subtitle. One space follows the colon. Alternatively, the subtitle may be set in a smaller size font than that of the main title (no colon).

> *Skating on Thin Ice: A Study of Honesty in Political Campaigning*
>
> *Skating on Thin Ice*
>
> *A Study of Honesty in Political Campaigning*

1.55   **tables**. Tables permit the economical presentation of large amounts of information. Number all tables and refer to them in the text by those numbers, either directly or parenthetically. In referring to a table, don't just repeat the facts presented in the table. Most of the time, a simple cross-reference is sufficient (see table 10). Number the tables (with Arabic numerals) in the order in which they appear in the text. Numbering is continuous throughout the text. However, if a book consists of chapters by different authors, the numbering restarts with each chapter (e.g., 1.1, 1.2, 2.1, 2.2, 3.1, 3.2, etc.). If a book has appendixes with tables, the table numbers should include the letter of the particular appendix (A.1, A.2, B.1, B.2, C.1, C.2, etc.).

Place the title above the table, flush left with the table, following the number, separated by punctuation or by space and typographic distinction. Use sentence-style capitalization; if the author and editor prefer, headline-style is also acceptable (one style should be used consistently throughout the text). Alternatively (and less commonly), the number may appear on a line by itself, with the title starting a new line (*Chicago*, 13.16, 13.18):

> Table 3. Army and air component budgets, 1922–41
>
> **TABLE 3** Army and air component budgets, 1922–41
>
> **Table 6**
> Army officer manning between the world wars

Note that the table designation and caption/legend may be set in boldface:

> **Table 2. Two assessment information requirements**

The title should identify the table and give facts rather than provide discussion and comment:

> Table 3. Improvement of prediction of peer leadership characteristics
>
> *Not:*
>
> Table 3. Improvement of prediction of peer leadership characteristics by addition of other managerial leadership characteristics

If the table continues to other pages, use a notation such as Table 3 (*continued*) at the top of the next page. Parenthetical information included in the title should be lowercased:

Table 13. Federal employees in the progressive era (total plus selected agencies)

A table must have at least two columns. At the top of the columns, include headings that identify the material in the columns. Do not use vertical rules to separate the columns. Make the first column heading singular in number (e.g., Party). The other headings may be singular or plural (e.g., Votes, Seats won). Preferably, all headings should be in sentence-style capitalization. If you include subheadings with the column headings, enclose them in parentheses. You may use abbreviations in the subheadings. Because the width of the column headings determines the width of the table, keep the headings as brief as possible.

List the names of items in the left-hand column (stub) of your table; use sentence-style capitalization and put information about them in the other columns. Be sure that items in the stub are grammatically parallel. Do not number stub items, and do not use ditto marks in the stub. Indent run-over lines one em. Write stub items in sentence style, without a period at the end:

Computers at headquarters
  Zenith
  Gateway
  IBM

Printers at headquarters
  Hewlett-Packard
  Epson
  Star

If you use the word Total *at the foot of the stub, indent it more deeply than the greatest indention above it or distinguish it typographically (Chicago, 13.29).*

Align a column of figures on the decimal points or commas. Also align dollar signs and percentage signs. If all figures in a column are the same kind, place the dollar signs and percentage signs only at the top of the column and after any horizontal rule cutting across it. Omit the signs if the table title or column head shows what the figures are.

In a column consisting of information expressed in words, center all items if they are short, but flush them left if they are long.

If you wish to refer to specific parts of a table, use superior letters—beginning with *a*—as reference marks. You may use them on column headings, on stub items, and in the body of the table—but not on the table number or title. Place the reference marks beginning at the upper left and extending across the table and downward, row by row. If you reproduce a table from another source, identify it below the body of the table, introduced by the word *Source(s)* (often in italics and followed by a colon). Since the word *source* lacks specificity, consider using *reprinted from* or *adapted from*, depending upon whether you have copied the table or modified it, respectively. *Unless fair use applies [see appendix C], a table reproduced without change from a published work under copyright requires formal permission (Chicago, 13.45).* Do not identify the source by placing a note number after either the table number or the title and then including an endnote in the list of chapter notes. *A note applying to the table as a whole follows any source note, is unnumbered, and is introduced by the word* Note *and a colon (often in italics) (Chicago, 13.46).*

If a book has either very many or very few tables, it is not necessary to include a list of them. Multiauthor books, a collection of symposia proceedings, and so forth do not usually include lists of tables (Chicago, 1.44). If such a list is included, it follows the list of illustrations, if there is one. Although tables are not considered illustrations, they may occasionally be listed under a subhead in the list of illustrations (e.g., if space so dictates) (Chicago, 1.47).

Table 1. Sorties flown in Operation Desert Storm

Sortie	*Allies*	*USAF*	*Other US*	*Total Coalition*
AI[a]	4,600	24,000	11,900	40,500
OCA[b]	1,400	4,500	600	6,500
CAS[c]	0	1,500	1,500	3,000
Total strike sorties[d]	6,000	30,000	14,000	50,000
Aerial refueling	1,500	10,000	1,500	13,000
DCA[e]	4,100	3,200	2,700	10,000
SEAD[f]	0	2,800	1,200	4,000
Tactical airlift	4,300	14,000	0	18,300
Other[g]	1,100	6,000	7,900	15,000
Total nonstrike sorties	11,000	36,000	13,300	60,300
Approximate grand total of all Desert Storm sorties				110,300

Reprinted from Department of the Air Force, *Air Force Performance in Desert Storm* (Washington, DC [or D.C.]: Government Printing Office, April 1991); and author's collation of published data.

Note: These figures represent the most reliable information currently available.

[a]Air interdiction—in this case a conflation of both strategic (against Iraqi installations) and operational (against Iraqi air, ground, and naval forces) bombing, including battlefield interdiction (against Iraqi forces behind the front).

[b]Offensive counterair (i.e., attacks against Iraqi air force bases and related facilities).

[c]Close air support (i.e., attacks against Iraqi ground forces at the front).

[d]*Strike* as here defined includes all aircraft that penetrated hostile airspace in the course of ground-attack missions, *with or without* ground-attack ordnance of their own.

[e]Defensive counterair (i.e., air defense patrols and intercepts).

[f]Suppression of enemy air defenses (i.e., attacks against Iraqi antiaircraft missiles, guns, and related radar and other facilities).

[g]Airborne early warning, airborne electronic surveillance, electronic warfare, and other.

1.56 **the**. If an initial *the* is part of the titles of journals, magazines, or newspapers, incorporate it into the surrounding text:

> Most of the people in the office read the *Wall Street Journal.*

Omit an initial *the* in note and bibliography entries:

> 1. Cameron W. Barr, "Mideast Takes a First Wary Step," *Christian Science Monitor,* 30 June 2003.

See also abbreviations (2.0).

1.57 **trademarks**. The symbols ® and ™, which often accompany registered trademark names on product packaging and in advertisements, need not be used in running text.

1.58 **Truman, Harry S.** Use a period after the initial *S.*

1.59 **United States**. Spell out *United States* in text when it is used as a noun. See also abbreviations (2.0); US (United States) (2.426).

1.60 **United States Air Force, US Air Force, Air Force, USAF**. See also USAF (United States Air Force) (2.428).

1.61 **United States Army, US Army, Army, USA**

1.62 **United States Marine Corps, US Marine Corps, Marine Corps, the Corps, USMC**

1.63 **United States Navy, US Navy, Navy, USN**

1.64 **upon** (prep.). *Upon* may be used as a synonym of *on*: His salary depends upon his performance.

1.65 **vice** (prep.). *Vice* can mean "in place of, replacing": John Doe was appointed postmaster vice Richard Roe.

1.66 **weapon system(s) or weapons system(s)**. Choose one variant of this phrase, and use it consistently.

1.67 **Web address**. See URL (uniform [or universal] resource locator) (2.425); see also Web, Web site, Web-site (adj.) (4.1.153).

1.68 **West Berlin, West Germany**. Use *West Berlin or West Germany*, not *Berlin* or *Germany* alone, in references to the city and country when they were divided.

1.69   **while**. You may use this term to mean "during the time that":

> Take a nap while I'm out.

or "as long as":

> While there's life, there's hope.

or "whereas":

> Skiing is easy for an expert, while it is dangerous for a novice.

or "although":

> While respected, he is not liked.

or "similarly and at the same time that":

> While the book will be welcomed by scholars, it will make an immediate appeal to the general reader.

1.70   **white (people)**. Use white (or White) officer, white (or White) people, whites (or Whites), Caucasians. See also black (people) (1.17); Negro, Negroes (1.39).

1.71   **word division**. Generally, you should follow the syllable division indicated in the dictionary when you break words at the ends of lines. Note the following prohibitions: do not carry over a final syllable whose only vowel sound is that of a syllabic "l" (prin-ciples, *not* princi-ples); do not carry over a vowel that forms a syllable in the middle of a word (preju-dice, *not* prej-udice); do not divide a word if doing so would result in a one-letter division (e.g., again, idol, item, unite); avoid carrying over two-letter endings (fully, *not* ful-ly); if possible, do not break hyphenated compound words except at the hyphen (court-/martial, *not* court-mar-/tial); words originally compounds of other words but now spelled solid should be divided at the natural breaks whenever possible (school-master *is better than* schoolmas-ter); also, try to make a division after a prefix rather than dividing at any other point in the word (dis-pleasure *is better than* displea-sure). Do not end more than three succeeding lines in hyphens.

1.72   **World War I (or 1), the First World War, the Great War, the war, the world war**

1.73   **World War II (or 2), the Second World War, the war, the world war**

1.74 **Xerox**. The term *Xerox* is a registered trademark. You can use the capitalized word as a noun meaning a xerographic copier and the lowercased word *(xerox)* as a verb meaning to copy on a Xerox copier.

1.75 **zero, zeros (also zeroes)**. Use a 0 in tables to denote zero amount instead of using a dash or leaving the space blank.

1.76 **zip code or ZIP (zone improvement plan) code; zip** (n.); **zip-code** (v.). In writing a mailing address, do not use a comma before the ZIP code (or after, if including "USA"): Troy, AL 36081 USA.

2.0   Abbreviations

"Abbreviations" is an inclusive term for "acronyms" (terms based on the initial letters of words and read as single words [NATO, NORAD]), "initialisms" (terms read as a series of letters [NBC, ISR]), and "contractions" (terms consisting of the first and last letters of full words [Mr., Dr.]), as well as other shortened forms of words (*Chicago*, 15.3). Use abbreviations sparingly: don't abbreviate words and phrases merely for the sake of doing so when brevity is not of the essence, and don't saturate writing with abbreviations to the detriment of reader comprehension.

Avoid using abbreviations in headings unless the spelled-out term would make the heading unwieldy. You may, however, begin or end a sentence with an abbreviation.

Spell out the name of an agency, organization, and so forth, the first time you use it, and follow it with the abbreviation in parentheses; you may use the abbreviation (without periods) thereafter (if you are certain that your audience is familiar with a particular abbreviation [e.g., AFB, USAF], you need not define it on first usage):

> North Atlantic Treaty Organization (NATO)
> Air Command and Staff College (ACSC)
> Internal Revenue Service (IRS)
> Cable News Network (CNN)
> program evaluation review technique (PERT)
> professional military education (PME)

As a reminder to the reader, you may want to spell out an abbreviation that you have identified previously—especially when you haven't used it in a long time—and then resume using the abbreviation (it isn't necessary to include it again parenthetically after the subsequent spelled-out form):

> The Pioneer unmanned aerial vehicle provided substantial imagery support to Marine, Army, and Navy units during Operation Desert Storm. These UAVs were so good that many more could have been used.

Because readers may not look at the elements of the front matter consecutively (if at all), establish abbreviations within each element (foreword, preface, abstract, etc.). For example, even if you have established "AWACS" in the foreword (e.g., Airborne Warning and Control System [AWACS]), reestablish this abbreviation if it occurs later in the front matter (e.g., in the preface). Reestablish abbreviations starting in the body of the publication (e.g., first chapter, section, part, etc.) even though they appear in the front matter. The same principle holds true for elements of the back matter and for a book collection of essays by different authors. For example, reestablish abbreviations in an appendix even if you have used them in the front matter or body and reestablish abbreviations in each essay even if you have used them in other essays in the book.

Although a term may be plural or possessive, do not make the abbreviation plural or possessive on first usage: cluster bomb units (CBU); low noise amplifiers (LNA). Use the plural or possessive form for subsequent occurrences of the abbreviation, when appropriate: CBUs, LNA's.

Even though an abbreviation may stand for a plural term (e.g., precision-guided munitions [PGM]), consider the abbreviation itself a singular noun: PGMs (plural), PGM's (possessive), the PGM *is* (not *are*).

Generally, use *the* with an abbreviation if you would use it with the spelled-out term in the particular context in which it appears, unless the combination seems awkward:

> He works for the DOD.
> The city is home to many DOD employees.
> NATO found itself at a crossroads.

Use capital letters for the abbreviations of computer-file extensions such as PDF, GIF, and JPG (or JPEG) unless they are actually appended to file names (f22.jpg).

Italicize an abbreviation only if it would be italicized if spelled out (*Chicago*, 15.8):

> *Oxford English Dictionary (OED)*
> *Journal of the American Medical Association (JAMA)*

Spell out the names of countries in text when they are used as nouns (however, you may use USSR [Union of Soviet Socialist Republics] to refer to the country as it existed between 1917 and 1991). If space is a consideration, you may abbreviate the names of countries in tables, lists, notes, and so forth. See also CIS (Commonwealth of Independent States) (2.92); US (United States) (2.426); USSR (Union of Soviet Socialist Republics) (2.444).

> United States (US)
> United Arab Emirates (UAE)
> United Kingdom (UK)
> France (Fr.)
> Germany (Ger.)
> Israel (Isr.)

Abbreviate civilian and military titles or ranks that precede a person's full name. Do not use periods with military ranks. Spell out titles or ranks that precede a person's last name only (see also military titles and offices [2.258]):

Adm Chester W. Nimitz	Admiral Nimitz
Vice Adm John Smith	Admiral Smith
Rear Adm Michael Wiggins	Admiral Wiggins
Cdr Henry Price	Commander Price
Air Chief Marshal Sir Arthur Harris	Marshal Harris
Gen Richard B. Myers	General Myers

Brig Gen James Stewart	General Stewart
Lt Col Martin L. Green	Colonel Green
Maj Frank T. Boothe	Major Boothe
Capt Donald D. Martin	Captain Martin
1st Lt Peter N. Cushing	Lieutenant Cushing
2d (or 2nd) Lt Boyd D. Yeats	Lieutenant Yeats
CMSgt Robert Patterson	Chief Patterson
MSgt Walter Austin	Sergeant Austin
A1C K. L. Jones	Airman Jones
Prof. Harold Bloom	Professor Bloom
Assoc. Prof. John Cooper	Professor Cooper
Asst. Prof. Dwight Hicks	Professor Hicks
Gov. Bob Riley	Governor Riley
Pres. George W. Bush	President Bush
Amb. John D. Negroponte	Ambassador Negroponte
Rep. Terry Everett (R-Ala. [or AL])	Representative Everett
Cong. Robert Cramer (D-Ala. [or AL])	Congressman Cramer
but Senator Jon Kyl (R-Ariz. [or AZ])	Senator Kyl
Rev. John Brannon	the Reverend John Brannon
Hon. James Lunsford	the Honorable James Lunsford

Always abbreviate social titles whether they precede the full name or last name only: Mr., Mrs., Messrs., Mr., Dr. When Mister or Doctor is used without a name, in direct address, spell it out (Chicago, 15.16).

Spell out a unit of measure on first usage, follow it with the abbreviation in parentheses, and use the abbreviation thereafter. *In nonscientific copy, periods customarily accompany English units of measure (e.g., lb., mi., in., ft. cu. in., qt., gal.) (Chicago 15.71).* Capitalize abbreviations for terms derived from proper names (e.g., Hz). Singular and plural abbreviated forms for units of measure are the same (e.g., 5 lb.). See also numbers (4.3).

gallon	gal.
hertz	Hz
kilogram	kg
miles per hour	mph
degrees Celsius	70° C
revolutions per minute	rpm
kilometer	km
millimeter	mm
pounds per square inch	psi
nautical mile	nm

Spell out the names of states, territories, and possessions of the United States in textual material. When the names appear in lists, tabular matter, notes, bibliographies, and indexes, use either the older forms of state abbreviations or the two-letter, no-period state abbreviations preferred by the US Postal Service (Chicago, 15.29). Choose one system, and use it consistently:

Ala. (AL)	Kans. (KS)	N.Dak. (ND)
Alaska (AK)	Ky. (KY)	Ohio (OH)

Amer. Samoa (AS)	La. (LA)	Okla. (OK)
Ariz. (AZ)	Maine (ME)	Oreg. or Ore. (OR)
Ark. (AR)	Md. (MD)	Pa. (PA)
Calif. (CA)	Mass. (MA)	P.R. (PR)
Colo. (CO)	Mich. (MI)	R.I. (RI)
Conn. (CT)	Minn. (MN)	S.C. (SC)
Del. (DE)	Miss. (MS)	S.Dak. (SD)
D.C. (DC)	Mo. (MO)	Tenn. (TN)
Fla. (FL)	Mont. (MT)	Tex. (TX)
Ga. (GA)	Nebr. (NE)	Utah (UT)
Guam (GU)	Nev. (NV)	Vt. (VT)
Hawaii (HI)	N.H. (NH)	Va. (VA)
Idaho (ID)	N.J. (NJ)	V.I. (VI)
Ill. (IL)	N.Mex. (NM)	Wash. (WA)
Ind. (IN)	N.Y. (NY)	W.Va. (WV)
Iowa (IA)	N.C. (NC)	Wis. or Wisc. (WI)
		Wyo. (WY)

In notes, bibliographies, and reference lists, you may use abbreviations freely, but be consistent. You may also use abbreviated forms in parenthetical references. Use the following terms: vol. 1, bk. 1, pt. 2, no. 2, chap. 2, fig. 4, art. 3, sec. 4, par. 5, col. 6, p. 7, n.d. (no date). The plurals are vols., bks., pts., nos., chaps., figs., arts., secs., pars., cols., pp.

2.1   **AAA (antiaircraft artillery)**

2.2   **AAM (air-to-air missile)**

2.3   **AB (air base).** Cite a first reference to a specific air base as follows: Rhein-Main Air Base (AB), Germany. Subsequent references: Rhein-Main AB, Germany; the air base; the base.

2.4   **ABCCC (airborne battlefield command and control center)**

2.5   **ABM (antiballistic missile)**

2.6   **academic degrees and titles.** Abbreviate academic degrees and titles (no periods) after a personal name. See also associate's degree (4.1.22); bachelor's degree (4.1.23); doctorate (4.1.55); master's degree (4.1.97).

BA
MA
PhD
LLD
MD
DDS
JP (justice of the peace)
MP (member of Parliament)

2.7   **ACC (Air Combat Command)**

2.8   **ACSC (Air Command and Staff College)**

2.9 **AD (anno Domini).** Use either small caps with or without periods or full caps without periods (choose one style, and use it consistently); the abbreviation precedes the year: AD 107. See also BC (before Christ) (2.65, 4.1.26).

2.10 **ADVON (advanced echelon)**

2.11 **AEF (air and space expeditionary force)**

2.12 **AEG (air expeditionary group)**

2.13 **AETC (Air Education and Training Command)**

2.14 **AETF (air and space expeditionary task force)**

2.15 **AEW (airborne early warning; air expeditionary wing)**

2.16 **AFB (Air Force base).** Because of its familiarity, you need not spell out this abbreviation on first usage: Maxwell AFB, Alabama. Subsequent references: the Air Force base; the base. In notes and bibliographies, abbreviate the name of the state: Maxwell AFB, AL (or Ala.).

2.17 **AFCC (Air Force component commander)**

2.18 **AFCERT (Air Force computer emergency response team)**

2.19 **AFDC (Air Force Doctrine Center)**

2.20 **AFDD (Air Force doctrine document)**

2.21 **AFFOR (Air Force forces)**

2.22 **AFHRA (Air Force Historical Research Agency)**

2.23 **AFI (Air Force instruction)**

2.24 **AFIADL (Air Force Institute for Advanced Distributed Learning)**

2.25 **AFIT (Air Force Institute of Technology)**

2.26 **AFLC (Air Force Logistics Command)**

2.27 **AFMAN (Air Force manual)**

2.28 **AFMC (Air Force Materiel Command)**

2.29 **AFOATS (Air Force Officer Accession and Training Schools)**

2.30 **AFOSI (Air Force Office of Special Investigations)**

2.31 **AFPAM (Air Force pamphlet)**

2.32 **AFPD (Air Force policy directive)**

2.33 **AFRC (Air Force Reserve Command)**. See also Reserve(s) (4.1.125).

2.34 **AFROTC (Air Force Reserve Officer Training Corps)**

2.35 **AFSOC (Air Force Special Operations Command)**

2.36 **AFSPC (Air Force Space Command)**

2.37 **AFTTP (Air Force tactics, techniques, and procedures)**

2.38 **AF/XO (Deputy Chief of Staff for Plans and Operations, USAF)**

2.39 **AF/XOI (Air Force Director of Intelligence, Surveillance, and Reconnaissance)**

2.40 **AI (air interdiction)**

2.41 **AIDS (acquired immunodeficiency syndrome)**

2.42 **ALCM (air launched cruise missile)**

2.43 **a.m. (ante meridiem [before noon])**. Either write the abbreviation in lowercase with periods or set it in small caps without periods (choose one style and use it consistently): 9:00 a.m.

2.44 **AMC (Air Mobility Command)**

2.45 **ampersand (&)**. Change an ampersand in original titles to *and (Aviation Week and Space Technology)*. Consistently use either the ampersand or *and* as it appears in company names in notes, bibliographies, lists, and parenthetical references (Harper & Row, Harper and Row), but use *and* in running text. The ampersand also occurs in some abbreviations: R&D (no space on either side of the ampersand in such abbreviations).

2.46 **AMRAAM (advanced medium-range air-to-air missile)**

2.47 **ANG (Air National Guard)**. Capitalize the shortened title: the Guard, but guardsman.

2.48 **AO (area of operations)**

2.49 **AOC (air and space operations center)**

2.50 **AOR (area of responsibility)**

2.51 **ARM (antiradiation missile)**

2.52 **ARNG (Army National Guard)**. Shortened form: the Guard.

2.53 **ASAP (as soon as possible)**

2.54 **ASAT (antisatellite weapon)**

2.55 **ASBC (Air and Space Basic Course)**

2.56 **ATACMS (Army Tactical Missile System)**

2.57 **ATAF (Allied Tactical Air Force [NATO])**

2.58 **ATO (air tasking order)**

2.59 **AU (Air University)**

2.60 **AUL (Air University Library)**

2.61 **AWACS (Airborne Warning and Control System)**

2.62 **AWC (Air War College)**

2.63 **AWOL (absent without leave)**

2.64 **base**. See AB (air base) (2.3); AFB (Air Force base) (2.16).

2.65 **BC (before Christ)**. Use either small caps with or without periods or full caps without periods (choose one style, and use it consistently); the abbreviation follows the year: 240 BC. See also AD (anno Domini) (2.9, 4.1.5).

2.66 **BCE (before the common era)**. See also CE (2.85).

> *Herod Antipas (21 BCE–39 CE) was tetrarch of Galilee from 4 BCE until his death. (Chicago, 9.38)*

2.67 **BDA (battle damage assessment)**

2.68 **BMD (ballistic missile defense)**

2.69 **BMDO (Ballistic Missile Defense Organization)**

2.70 **BRAC (base realignment and closure)**

2.71 **BVR (beyond visual range)**

2.72   C² or C2 (command and control)

2.73   C³ or C3 (command, control, and communications)

2.74   C³I or C3I (command, control, communications, and intelligence)

2.75   C⁴ or C4 (command, control, communications, and computers)

2.76   C⁴I or C4I (command, control, communications, computers, and intelligence)

2.77   CADRE (College of Aerospace Doctrine, Research and Education)

2.78   CALCM (conventional air-launched cruise missile)

2.79   CAOC (combat [or combined] air operations center) [Joint Pub 1-02]; (combat [or combined] air and space operations center) [USAF]

2.80   CAP (Civil Air Patrol; combat air patrol; crisis action planning)

2.81   CAS (close air support)

2.82   CBU (cluster bomb unit)

2.83   CBW (chemical and biological warfare)

2.84   CCAF (Community College of the Air Force)

2.85   CE (of the common era). See also BCE (2.66)

> *Herod Antipas (21 BCE–39 CE) was tetrarch of Galilee from 4 BCE until his death. (Chicago, 9.38)*

2.86   CEPME (College for Enlisted Professional Military Education)

2.87   CFACC (combined force air component commander) [Joint Pub 1-02]; (combined force air and space component commander) [USAF]

2.88   **chapter.** Abbreviate *chapter* in parenthetical references (chap. 5). Lowercase and spell out the word in text. Use Arabic figures for chapter numbers, even if the chapter numbers in the work cited are spelled out or in Roman numerals. The same principle holds true for other divisions of a book: part 1, section 3, book 7, volume 2.

2.89 **CHOP (change of operational control)**

2.90 **CIA (Central Intelligence Agency)**

2.91 **CINC (commander in chief).** Use only in reference to the president of the United States. Use *commander of a combatant command* in reference to leaders of combatant or unified commands (e.g., commander of US Central Command).

2.92 **CIS (Commonwealth of Independent States).** The free association of sovereign states formed in 1991, comprising Russia and 11 other republics formerly part of the Soviet Union. See also Soviet(s), Soviet Union, USSR (1.52).

2.93 **CJCS (chairman of the Joint Chiefs of Staff)**

2.94 **CNA (computer network attack)**

2.95 **CNO (chief of naval operations)**

2.96 **CO (commanding officer)**

2.97 **COC (combat operations center)**

2.98 **COG (center of gravity)**

2.99 **COMAFFOR (commander, Air Force forces)**

2.100 **COMPUSEC (computer security)**

2.101 **COMSAT (communications satellite)**

2.102 **CONOPS (concept of operations)**

2.103 **CONUS (continental United States)**

2.104 **CRAF (civil reserve air fleet)**

2.105 **CSAF (chief of staff, United States Air Force)**

2.106 **CSAR (combat search and rescue)**

2.107 **CV (aircraft carrier; carrier)**

2.108 **CW (chemical warfare)**

2.109 **DARPA (Defense Advanced Research Projects Agency)**

2.110 DC or D.C. (District of Columbia)

2.111 DEA (Drug Enforcement Administration)

2.112 DEFCON (defense readiness condition)

2.113 DET (detachment)

2.114 DFAS (Defense Finance and Accounting Service)

2.115 DHS (Department of Homeland Security)

2.116 DIA (Defense Intelligence Agency)

2.117 DMPI (designated [or desired] mean point of impact)

2.118 DMSP (Defense Meteorological Satellite Program)

2.119 DMZ (demilitarized zone)

2.120 **doctrine documents, instructions, manuals, pamphlets, and policy directives**. On first usage, spell out the type of publication (doctrine document, instruction, etc.) and follow it with the abbreviation in parentheses; use the abbreviation and number for subsequent references. Italicize the title of the publication: Air Force Doctrine Document (AFDD) 2-4.3, *Education and Training*, AFDD 2-4.3; Air Force Instruction (AFI) 90-201, *Inspector General Activities*, AFI 90-201; Air Force Manual (AFMAN) 10-100, *Airman's Manual*, AFMAN 10-100; Army Field Manual (FM) 27-10, *The Law of Land Warfare*, FM 27-10; Air Force Pamphlet (AFPAM) 36-2705, *Discrimination and Sexual Harassment*, AFPAM 36-2705; Air Force Policy Directive (AFPD) 36-4, *Air Force Civilian Training and Education*, AFPD 36-4.

2.121 DOD (Department of Defense)

2.122 DODD (Department of Defense directive)

2.123 DODI (Department of Defense instruction)

2.124 DODM (Department of Defense manual)

2.125 DODR (Department of Defense regulation)

2.126 **Dr.** (doctor). Use a period with the abbreviation. See also abbreviations (2.0); Mr., Mrs., Mme, Ms. (2.269); Messrs., Mmes. (2.252).

2.127 **DRU (direct reporting unit)**

2.128 **DSN (Defense Switched Network)**

2.129 **EAF (expeditionary air and space forces)**

2.130 **EBO (effects-based operations)**

2.131 **e.g. (for example).** Avoid using *e.g.* in text; use *for example* instead. Use the abbreviation, followed by a comma, only in parenthetical references or tabular matter.

2.132 **ELINT (electronic intelligence)**

2.133 **EO (executive order).** Lowercase and spell out *executive order* in general references when the number is not given: the executive order. Always capitalize the term when a number accompanies it, but abbreviate the term with the number only after spelling it out on first reference: Executive Order (EO) 1654, EO 1654, the executive order.

2.134 **et al. (and others).** *Et al.* follows the full name of the first author listed in a note reference to a work by more than three authors:

> 1. Jaroslav Pelikan et al., *Religion and the University*, York University Invitation Lecture Series (Toronto: University of Toronto Press, 1964), 109.

2.135 **etc. (and so forth).** The spelled-out term *et cetera* is rarely used. Use its abbreviation, *etc.*, only in lists, tables, and parenthetical references. Use *and so forth* in running text, set off by commas.

> Joan had a variety of candy bars in her purse (Baby Ruths, Snickers, Mounds, etc.).
>
> The animal shelter offered such dogs as terriers, Pomeranians, Chihuahuas, and so forth, for adoption.

2.136 **EU (European Union)**

2.137 **EW (early warning; electronic warfare)**

2.138 **FAC (forward air controller)**

2.139 **FBI (Federal Bureau of Investigation)**

2.140 **FBIS (Foreign Broadcast Information Service)**

2.141 **FEBA (forward edge of the battle area)**

2.142   FEMA (Federal Emergency Management Agency)

2.143   FLIR (forward-looking infrared)

2.144   FLOT (forward line of own troops)

2.145   FM (field manual [Army])

2.146   FOA (field operating agency)

2.147   FOIA (Freedom of Information Act)

2.148   FOUO (for official use only)

2.149   FP (force protection)

2.150   FPCON (force protection condition)

2.151   FRAG (fragmentation code)

2.152   frequencies. See abbreviations (2.0).

2.153   FS (fighter squadron)

2.154   FSCL (fire support coordination line)

2.155   FW (fighter wing)

2.156   FY (fiscal year). FY 2004, FY 04.

2.157   GAO (Government Accountability Office)

2.158   GBU (guided bomb unit)

2.159   GCA (ground controlled approach)

2.160   GCI (ground control intercept)

2.161   general (military rank). See abbreviations (2.0); capitalization (4.1); military titles and offices (2.258).

2.162   GEO (geosynchronous Earth orbit)

2.163   g-force

2.164   GHz (gigahertz)

2.165 **GLCM (ground launched cruise missile)**

2.166 **GMT (Greenwich Mean Time)**

2.167 **GO (general order).** Lowercase and spell out *general order* in references when the number is not given: the general order. Capitalize the term when a number accompanies it, but abbreviate the term with the number only after spelling it out on first reference: General Order (GO) 6-325, GO 6-325, the general order.

2.168 **GPS (global positioning system)**

2.169 **GSA (General Services Administration)**

2.170 **G suit**

2.170.1 GWOT (global war on terrorism)

2.171 **HARM (high-speed antiradiation missile)**

2.172 **HF (high frequency)**

2.173 **H hour (specific time when an operation or exercise begins)**

2.174 **HIV (human immunodeficiency virus)**

2.175 **HMMWV (high mobility multipurpose wheeled vehicle)**

2.176 **HMW (health, morale, and welfare)**

2.177 **HRO (humanitarian relief organizations)**

2.178 **HUD (head-up display)**

2.179 **HUMINT (human intelligence)**

2.180 **HUMRO (humanitarian relief operation)**

2.181 **Hz (hertz)**

2.182 **IA (information attack or information assurance)**

2.183 **IADS (Integrated Air Defense System)**

2.184 **ibid. (in the same place).** *The abbreviation "ibid." ("ibidem," "in the same place") refers to a single work cited in the note immediately preceding. Never use "ibid." if more than one work is cited in the* *preceding note* (*Chicago*, 16.47). Do not italicize this abbreviation in your notes. Do not use *op. cit.* (*opere citato*, "in the work cited") or *loc. cit.* (*loco citato*, "in the place cited"). Instead, use the shortened form of the citation. *You may use "ibid." within the note to indicate successive references to the same work (*Chicago*, 16.48).*

> 7. Richard G. Davis, *Carl A. Spaatz and the Air War in Europe* (Washington, DC [or D.C.]: Office of Air Force History, 1993), 331.
> 8. Ibid., 301.
> 9. Gen Richard B. Myers, "A Word from the Chairman: Shift to a Global Perspecitve," *Air and Space Power Journal* 17, no. 3 (Fall 2003): 5. "By shifting our view from a regional to a global perspective, we will better comprehend and respond to America's security needs in the twenty-first century" (ibid., 8).

2.185   ICBM (intercontinental ballistic missile)

2.186   i.e. (that is). Avoid using *i.e.* in running text; use *that is* instead. Use the abbreviation, followed by a comma, only in parenthetical references or tabular matter.

2.187   IEEE (Institute of Electrical and Electronics Engineers)

2.188   IFF (identification, friend or foe)

2.189   IG (inspector general)

2.190   IMA (individual mobilization augmentee)

2.191   IMINT (imagery intelligence)

2.192   INFOCON (information operations condition)

2.193   INFOSEC (information security)

2.194   INS (inertial navigation system)

2.195   INTELSAT (International Telecommunications Satellite Organization)

2.196   IO (information operations)

2.197   I/O (input/output)

2.198   IOS (International Officer School)

2.199   IR (infrared)

2.200 ISR (intelligence, surveillance, and reconnaissance)

2.201 IW (information warfare)

2.202 I&W (indications and warning)

2.203 J-1 (manpower and personnel directorate of a joint staff)

2.204 J-2 (intelligence directorate of a joint staff)

2.205 J-3 (operations directorate of a joint staff)

2.206 J-4 (logistics directorate of a joint staff)

2.207 J-5 (plans directorate of a joint staff)

2.208 J-6 (command, control, communications, and computer systems directorate of a joint staff)

2.209 J-7 (Operational Plans and Joint Force Development, Joint Staff)

2.210 J-8 (Director for Force Structure, Resource, and Assessment, Joint Staff)

2.211 JAG (judge advocate general)

2.212 JAOC (joint air operations center) [Joint Pub 1-02]; (joint air and space operations center) [USAF]

2.213 JAOP (joint air operations plan) [Joint Pub 1-02]; (joint air and space operations plan) [USAF]

2.214 JASSM (Joint Air-to-Surface Standoff Missile)

2.215 JCS (Joint Chiefs of Staff). Shortened form: joint chiefs.

2.216 JDAM (Joint Direct Attack Munition)

2.217 JFACC (joint force air component commander) [Joint Pub 1-02]; (joint air and space component commander) [USAF]

2.218 JFC (joint force commander)

2.219 JFLCC (joint force land component commander)

2.220 JFMCC (joint force maritime component commander)

2.221 **JFSOCC (joint force special operations component commander)**

2.222 **JOC (joint operations center)**

2.223 **JP (joint publication)**

2.224 **Jr.** Use with a period. Commas are not required; if you do use commas, place one before and after the abbreviation. Select one style, and use it consistently. Use a comma before the abbreviation when the name is inverted (as in an index).

> James Adair Jr. is the mayor.
> James Adair, Jr., is the mayor.
> Adair, James, Jr.

2.225 **JSOW (joint standoff weapon)**

2.226 **JSTARS (Joint Surveillance Target Attack Radar System)**

2.227 **JTF (joint task force)**

2.228 **kg (kilogram)**

2.229 **kHz (kilohertz)**

2.230 **KIA (killed in action)**

2.231 **km (kilometer)**

2.232 **LANDSAT (land satellite)**

2.233 **LANTIRN (low-altitude navigation and targeting infrared for night)**

2.234 **latitude, longitude.** Spell out *latitude* and *longitude* in text or standing alone: longitude 80 degrees east; the polar latitudes, from 20° 50′ north latitude to 20° 50′ south latitude. In tables you may abbreviate as follows:

> lat 41°15′40″ N
> long 90°18′30″ W

2.235 **LEO (low Earth orbit)**

2.236 **LF (low frequency)**

2.237 **LGB (laser-guided bomb)**

2.238 LGM (laser-guided missile)

2.239 LGW (laser-guided weapon)

2.240 LIC (low intensity conflict)

2.241 LIMFAC (limiting factor)

2.242 LOC (line of communications)

2.243 loc. cit. *(loco citato)*. In the place cited. Use a shortened reference instead. See also notes (5.1).

2.244 LORAN (long-range aid to navigation)

2.245 MAAP (master air attack plan)

2.245.1 MAAS (master of airpower art and science [degree, School of Advanced Air and Space Studies]) [Press editors: spell out on first usage]. See also master's degree (4.1.97).

2.246 MAGTF (Marine air-ground task force)

2.247 MAJCOM (major command [USAF])

2.248 MANPADS (man-portable air defense system)

2.249 MAW (Marine aircraft wing)

2.250 MEDEVAC (medical evacuation)

2.251 MEO (medium Earth orbit)

2.252 Messrs., Mmes. *Messrs.* is the plural of *Mr.*; use a period: Messrs. Bailey, Bryant, and Richardson. *Mmes* is the plural of *madam* or *madame* or *Mrs.*; no period: Mmes Clark, O'Neal, and Terrell. See also Mr., Mrs., Mme, Ms. (2.269).

2.253 MET (mission essential task)

2.254 MHz (megahertz)

2.255 MIA (missing in action)

2.256 MiG(s). Capital *M*, lowercase *i*, capital *G*. Soviet aircraft developed by the design bureau of Gen Artem Mikoyan and Gen Mikhail Gurevich. Abbreviation derived from the transliteration *M*ikoyan *i G*urevich.

2.257 **military abbreviations**. See Joint Publication 1-02, *Department of Defense Dictionary of Military and Associated Terms.*

2.258 **military titles and offices**. Capitalize and abbreviate titles that precede full names; capitalize and spell out titles that precede surnames only. Lowercase and spell out titles following a personal name or used alone in place of a name:

> Gen Ulysses S. Grant, commander in chief of the Union army; General Grant; the commander in chief; the general

> Lt Col Antulio J. Echevarria II, USA; Colonel Echevarria; the colonel

> Gen Curtis E. LeMay, commander of Strategic Air Command; General LeMay; the general

> *But* General of the Army Douglas MacArthur; Douglas MacArthur, general of the Army; General MacArthur; the general

> Sgt Phyllis Forsman; a noncommissioned officer (NCO); Sergeant Forsman; the sergeant

> Adm Chester W. Nimitz; Admiral Nimitz, commander of the Pacific Fleet; the fleet admiral

> Col (Brig Gen–select) Peter D. Haynes; Brig Gen (sel) Peter D. Haynes

> Generals Eisenhower and Montgomery (but Army generals Patton and Bradley)

See also abbreviations (2.0); capitalization (4.1).

The following service-specific abbreviations for military rank are provided primarily for reference purposes. In the body of your text, for the sake of simplicity and uniformity, use the cap-and-lowercase style for all ranks, regardless of the service (e.g., Capt rather than CAPT [Navy]). If appropriate, however, you may use the all-caps style in the front and back matter and documentation of books, monographs, theses, and so forth; the same holds true of chapter bylines in a book by multiple authors and in the bylines and documentation of journal articles, as well as material other than the text of the articles (e.g., staff and editorial-board listings, letters to the editor, contributors section, etc.). The cap-and-lowercase variants, if any, are indicated parenthetically below:

Air Force		*Army*	
Gen	general	GEN (Gen)	general
Lt Gen	lieutenant general	LTG (Lt Gen)	lieutenant general
Maj Gen	major general	MG (Maj Gen)	major general
Brig Gen	brigadier general	BG (Brig Gen)	brigadier general
Col	colonel	COL (Col)	colonel
Lt Col	lieutenant colonel	LTC (Lt Col)	lieutenant colonel
Maj	major	MAJ (Maj)	major

Air Force		*Army*	
Capt	captain	CPT (Capt)	captain
1st Lt	first lieutenant	1LT (1st Lt)	first lieutenant
2d/2nd Lt	second lieutenant	2LT (2d/2nd Lt)	second lieutenant
CMSAF	chief master sergeant of the Air Force		
CMSgt	chief master sergeant	CW5	chief warrant officer 5
SMSgt	senior master sergeant	CW4	chief warrant officer 4
MSgt	master sergeant	CW3	chief warrant officer 3
TSgt	technical sergeant	CW2	chief warrant officer 2
SSgt	staff sergeant	CW1	chief warrant officer 1
SrA	senior Airman		
A1C	Airman first class	SMA	sergeant major of the Army
Amn	Airman	CSM	command sergeant major
AB	Airman basic	SGM	sergeant major
		1SG (1st Sgt)	first sergeant
		MSG (MSgt)	master sergeant
		PSG	platoon sergeant
		SFC	sergeant first class
		SSG (SSgt)	staff sergeant
		SP6	specialist 6
		SGT (Sgt)	sergeant
		SP5	specialist 5
		CPL (Cpl)	corporal
		SP4	specialist 4
		PFC (Pfc)	private first class
		PVT (Pvt)	private

Marine Corps		*Navy/Coast Guard*	
Gen	general	ADM (Adm)	admiral
Lt Gen	lieutenant general	VADM (Vice Adm)	vice admiral
Maj Gen	major general	RADM (Rear Adm)	rear admiral (O-8/O-7)
B Gen (Brig Gen)	brigadier general	CAPT (Capt)	captain
Col	colonel	CDR (Cdr)	commander
Lt Col	lieutenant colonel	LCDR (Lt Cdr)	lieutenant commander
Maj	major	LT (Lt)	lieutenant
Capt	captain	LTJG (Lt JG)	lieutenant junior grade
1st Lt	first lieutenant	ENS (Ensign)	ensign
2d/2nd Lt	second lieutenant		
CWO-5	chief warrant officer 5	CWO5	chief warrant officer 5
CWO-4	chief warrant officer 4	CWO4	chief warrant officer 4
CWO-3	chief warrant officer 3	CWO3	chief warrant officer 3
CWO-2	chief warrant officer 2	CWO2	chief warrant officer 2
CWO-1	chief warrant officer 1	MCPON	master chief petty officer of the Navy
Sgt Maj	sergeant major	MCPO	master chief petty officer
Mgy Sgt	master gunnery sergeant	SCPO	senior chief petty officer
1st Sgt	first sergeant	CPO	chief petty officer
MSgt	master sergeant	PO1	petty officer first class
GySgt	gunnery sergeant	PO2	petty officer second class
SSgt	staff sergeant	PO3	petty officer third class

Marine Corps		*Navy/Coast Guard*	
Sgt	sergeant	SN	seaman
Cpl	corporal	SA	seaman apprentice
LCpl	lance corporal	SR	seaman recruit
PFC (Pfc)	private first class		
Pvt	private		

2.259 **MIRV (multiple independently targeted reentry vehicle)** (n.,v.). MIRVed, MIRVing.

2.260 **MISREP (mission report)**

2.261 **MITRE Corp. (Massachusetts Institute of Technology Research Corporation)**

2.261.1 **MMOAS (master of military operational art and science [degree, Air Command and Staff College]) [Press editors: spell out on first usage]**. See also master's degree (4.1.97).

2.262 **MOA (memorandum of agreement)**

2.263 **MOE (measure of effectiveness)**

2.264 **months of the year**. Write exact dates in day-month-year sequence, without commas. Spell out the month, use figures for the day, and use a four-digit year. When you use only month and year, no commas are necessary.

> FDR referred to 7 December 1941 as a day that would live in infamy.
> The date March 2003 was special to her.

Do not use the all-numeral style for dates (3/11/50, etc.) in formal writing. However, in text discussing the events of [11 September 2001], the use of 9/11 is acceptable (Chicago, 6.115). If documentation, figures, and tables contain numerous dates, you may abbreviate certain months (Jan., Feb., Mar., Apr., May, June, July, Aug., Sept., Oct., Nov., Dec.) and use the day-month-year sequence without internal punctuation (7 Dec. 1941) to reduce clutter. Choose one style for the documentation, figures, and tables, and use it consistently. See also numbers (4.3).

2.265 **MOOTW (military operations other than war)**

2.266 **MOS (military occupational specialty)**

2.267 **MOU (memorandum of understanding)**

2.268 **mph (miles per hour)**

2.269 **Mr., Mrs., Mme, Ms.** Use a period with all except Mme. Spell out "Mister" when it connotes military rank: Mister Roberts. See also Messrs., Mmes (2.252).

2.270 **MRE (meal, ready to eat)**

2.270.1 MSS (master of strategic studies [degree, Air War College]) [Press editors: spell out on first usage]. See also master's degree (4.1.97).

2.271 **MTW (major theater war)**

2.272 **NAF (nonappropriated funds; numbered air force)**

2.273 **NASA (National Aeronautics and Space Administration)**

2.274 **NATO (North Atlantic Treaty Organization)**

2.275 **NAVSAT (navigation satellite)**

2.276 **NBC (nuclear, biological, and chemical)**

2.277 **NCA (National Command Authorities).** No longer used. Use *president* and/or *secretary of defense*, as appropriate.

2.278 **NCO (noncombat operations; noncommissioned officer)**

2.279 **NCOIC (noncommissioned officer in charge)**

2.280 **NDU (National Defense University)**

2.281 **NEA (northeast Asia)**

2.282 **NEO (noncombat evacuation operation)**

2.283 **NGA (National Geospatial-Intelligence Agency).** Formerly the National Imagery and Mapping Agency (NIMA).

2.284 **NGB (National Guard Bureau)**

2.285 **NGO (nongovernmental organization)**

2.286 **NIPRNET (Nonsecure Internet Protocol Router Network)**

2.287 **nm (nautical mile)**

2.288 **no.** Use a period after the abbreviation for *number.*

2.289 NOFORN (not releasable to foreign nationals)

2.290 NORAD (North American Aerospace Defense Command)

2.291 NOTAM (notice to Airmen)

2.292 NRO (National Reconnaissance Office)

2.293 NSA (National Security Agency)

2.294 NSC (National Security Council)

2.295 NVG (night vision goggle)

2.296 OCA (offensive counterair)

2.297 OCI (offensive counterinformation)

2.298 OCS (offensive counterspace)

2.299 OJT (on-the-job training)

2.300 OL (operating location)

2.301 O&M (operation and maintenance)

2.302 OMB (Office of Management and Budget)

2.303 OODA (observe, orient, decide, act)

2.304 op. cit. (*opere citato*). In the work cited. Use a shortened reference instead. See notes (5.1).

2.305 OPCON (operational control)

2.306 OPLAN (operation plan)

2.307 OPM (Office of Personnel Management)

2.308 OPORD (operation order)

2.309 OPR (office of primary responsibility)

2.310 OPTEMPO (operating tempo)

2.311 **OSD (Office of the Secretary of Defense)**

2.312 **OT&E (operational test and evaluation)**

2.313 **OTS (Officer Training School)**

2.314 **PA (Public Affairs)**

2.315 **PACAF (Pacific Air Forces)**

2.316 **page numbers.** You may either use the abbreviations *p.* and *pp.* (pages) to designate page numbers, or you may omit them—as long as you are consistent:

> 2. Lt Col Kenneth Keskel, "The Oath of Office: A Historical Guide to Moral Leadership," *Air and Space Power Journal* 16, no. 4 (Winter 2002): 48 (or p. 48), http://www.airpower.maxwell.af.mil/airchronicles/apj/apj02/win02/win02.pdf.

2.317 **PAWS (phased array warning system)**

2.318 **PCS (permanent change of station)**

2.319 **PGM (precision-guided munitions)**

2.320 **PIREP (pilot report)**

2.321 **PKO (peacekeeping operations)**

2.322 **p.m. (post meridiem [after noon]).** Either write the abbreviation in lowercase with periods, or set it in small caps without periods (choose one style, and use it consistently).

2.323 **PME (professional military education)**

2.324 **POC (point of contact)**

2.325 **POL (petroleum, oil, and lubricants)**

2.326 **POM (program objective memorandum)**

2.327 **POW (prisoner of war)**

2.328 **PPBS (Planning, Programming, and Budgeting System)**

2.329   **Prime BEEF (Prime Base Engineer Emergency Force)**

2.330   **PSYOP (psychological operations)**

2.331   **PSYWAR (psychological warfare)**

2.332   **pub (publication)**

2.333   **RAF (Royal Air Force [United Kingdom])**

2.334   **rank.** See military titles and offices (2.258).

2.335   **rates of speed, frequencies, and so forth.** See abbreviations (2.0); measurements (4.3.15); numbers (4.3).

2.336   **RCS (radar cross section)**

2.337   **R&D (research and development)**

2.338   **RDA (research, development, and acquisition)**

2.339   **RDT&E (research, development, test, and evaluation)**

2.340   **RECCE (reconnaissance)**

2.341   **RECON (reconnaissance)**

2.342   **RED HORSE (Rapid Engineers Deployable Heavy Operations Repair Squadron, Engineers)**

2.343   **RMA (revolution in military affairs)**

2.344   **ROE (rules of engagement)**

2.345   **ROK (Republic of Korea)**

2.346   **ROTC (Reserve Officer Training Corps)**

2.347   **RPV (remotely piloted vehicle)**

2.348   **RRF (rapid reaction force)**

2.349   **SAASS (School of Advanced Air and Space Studies)**

2.350 **SACEUR (Supreme Allied Command, Europe)**

2.351 **SACLANT (Supreme Allied Command, Atlantic)**

2.352 **SAF (secretary of the Air Force)**

2.353 **Saint.** When *Saint* is part of someone's name, follow that person's usage (e.g., as indicated in *Webster's New Biographical Dictionary*).

Marco de Saint-Hilaire   Barry St. Leger

Place-names with Saint *may be abbreviated or spelled out in text* (*Chicago* 15.32).

St. Louis or Saint Louis

2.354 **SAM (surface-to-air missile)**

2.355 **SAOC (sector air operations center)**

2.356 **SAR (search and rescue; synthetic aperture radar)**

2.357 **SATCOM (satellite communications)**

2.358 **SBIRS (space-based infrared system)**

2.359 **SBR (space-based radar)**

2.360 **SBSS (space-based space surveillance)**

2.361 **SDI (Strategic Defense Initiative)**

2.362 **SEA (Southeast Asia)**

2.363 **SEAD (suppression of enemy air defenses)**

2.364 **SEAL (sea-air-land team)**

2.365 **SHAPE (Supreme Headquarters Allied Powers, Europe)**

2.366 **SIGINT (signals intelligence)**

2.367 **SIOP (Single Integrated Operational Plan)**

2.368 **SIPRNET (Secret Internet Protocol Router Network)**

2.369 **SITREP (situation report)**

2.370 **SJA (staff judge advocate)**

2.371 **SLAM (standoff land attack missile)**

2.372 **SLAR (side-looking airborne radar)**

2.373 **SLBM (submarine-launched ballistic missile)**

2.374 **SLCM (sea-launched cruise missile)**

2.375 **SLOC (sea line of communications)**

2.376 **SO (special order)**. Lowercase and spell out *special order* in general references when the number is not given: the special order. Capitalize the term when a number accompanies it, but abbreviate the term with the number only after you spell it out on first reference: Special Order (SO) T-013, SO T-013, the special order.

2.377 **SOC (space operations center; special operations command; Squadron Officer College)**

2.378 **SOF (special operations forces)**

2.379 **SOP (standing [or standard] operating procedure)**

2.380 **SORTS (Status of Resources and Training System)**

2.381 **SOS (Squadron Officer School)**

2.382 **SP (security police)**

2.383 **SPINS (special instructions)**

2.384 **Sr.** Use with a period. Commas are not required; if you do use commas, place one before and after the abbreviation. Select one style, and use it consistently. Use a comma before the abbreviation when the name is inverted (as in an index).

> M. H. Abrahms Sr. lives at the end of the street.
>
> M. H. Abrahms, Sr., lives at the end of the street.
>
> Abrahms, M. H., Sr.

2.385 **SROE** (standing rules of engagement)

2.386 **SSA** (space situational awareness)

2.387 **SSBN** (fleet ballistic missile submarine)

2.388 **SSM** (surface-to-surface missile)

2.389 **SSN** (attack submarine, nuclear)

2.390 **state names.** See abbreviations (2.0).

2.391 **STO** (space tasking order)

2.392 **STOL** (short takeoff and landing)

2.393 **STOVL** (short takeoff and vertical landing aircraft)

2.394 **SWA** (Southwest Asia)

2.395 **TACAIR** (tactical air)

2.396 **TACP** (tactical air control party)

2.397 **TAF** (tactical air force)

2.398 **TAW** (tactical airlift wing)

2.399 **TBM** (tactical/theater ballistic missile)

2.400 **TDY** (temporary duty)

2.401 **T&E** (test and evaluation)

2.402 **TEMPEST** (telecommunications electronics material protected from emanating spurious transmissions; transient electromagnetic pulse emanation standard)

2.403 **TERCOM** (terrain contour matching)

2.404 **titles of persons and offices.** See capitalization (4.1); military titles and offices (2.258).

2.405 **TLAM** (Tomahawk land-attack missile)

2.406 **TMD (theater missile defense)**

2.407 **TO (technical order)**. Lowercase and spell out *technical order* in general references when the number is not given: the technical order. Always capitalize the term when a number accompanies it, but abbreviate the term only after spelling it out on first reference: Technical Order (TO) 00-25-4, TO 00-25-4.

2.408 **TOF (time of flight)**

2.409 **TOT (time on target)**

2.410 **TOW (tube launched, optically tracked, wire guided)**

2.411 **TPFDD (time-phased force and deployment data)**

2.412 **TPFDL (time-phased force and deployment list)**

2.413 **TRADOC (US Army Training and Doctrine Command)**

2.414 **TRS (tactical reconnaissance squadron)**

2.415 **TTP (tactics, techniques, and procedures)**

2.416 **UAV (unmanned aerial vehicle)**

2.417 *UCMJ (Uniform Code of Military Justice)*. See also italics (4.4).

2.418 **UCP (Unified Command Plan)**

2.419 **UHF (ultrahigh frequency)**

2.420 **UK (United Kingdom)**

2.421 **UMD (unit manning document)**

2.422 **UN (United Nations)**. The abbreviation can be used as either a noun or an adjective.

2.423 **UNICEF (United Nations Children's Fund)**

2.424 **UNPROFOR (United Nations protection force)**

2.425 **URL (uniform [or universal] resource locator)**. A string that identifies a resource in the World Wide Web. In a printed work, if you must break a URL, do so after a slash (single or double) if possible. Do not break after a dot since this looks like a period at the end of a line and might confuse the reader; rather, place the dot at the beginning of the next line. Do not hyphenate a word at the end of a line since some URLs contain hyphens as part of the address, and do not leave a hyphen that's part of a URL at the end of a line. Additionally, break *before* a tilde (~), a hyphen, a comma, an underline (_), a question mark, a number sign (#), or a percent symbol— or *before* or *after* an equals sign or an ampersand (&).

2.426 **US (United States)**. Use the abbreviation as an adjective only.

2.427 **USA (United States Army)**

2.428 **USAF (United States Air Force)**. Can be used as either a noun or an adjective (serving in the USAF; USAF people). See also United States Air Force, US Air Force, Air Force, USAF (1.60).

2.429 **USAFE (United States Air Forces in Europe)**

2.430 **USAFR (United States Air Force Reserve)**

2.431 *USC (United States Code)*

2.432 **USCENTAF (United States Central Command Air Forces)**

2.433 **USCENTCOM (United States Central Command)**

2.434 **USCG (United States Coast Guard)**

2.435 **USEUCOM (United States European Command)**

2.436 **USJFCOM (United States Joint Forces Command)**

2.437 **USMC (United States Marine Corps)**

2.438 **USN (United States Navy)**

2.439 *USSBS (United States Strategic Bombing Survey)*. Italicize in references to the published work. Initial caps in Roman type are appropriate in references to the project prior to publication: United States Strategic Bombing Survey (USSBS).

2.440 **USSOCOM (United States Special Operations Command)**

2.441 **USSOUTHAF (United States Air Force, Southern Command)**

2.442 **USSOUTHCOM (United States Southern Command)**

2.443 **USSPACECOM (United States Space Command)**

2.444 **USSR (Union of Soviet Socialist Republics).** Use *Union of Soviet Socialist Republics* and its abbreviation in references to the country as it existed between 1917 and 1991. The abbreviation can be used as either a noun or an adjective. See also CIS (Commonwealth of Independent States) (2.92); Soviet(s), Soviet Union, USSR (1.52).

2.445 **USSTRATCOM (United States Strategic Command)**

2.446 **USTRANSCOM (United States Transportation Command)**

2.447 **USW (undersea warfare)**

2.448 **UTC (unit type code)**

2.449 **v. (versus).** Use *v.* instead of *vs.* in names of legal cases; in other contexts, use *versus*. See also italics (4.4).

2.450 **VFR (visual flight rules)**

2.451 **VHF (very high frequency)**

2.452 **viz.** (videlicet; that is to say, namely)

2.453 **VLF (very low frequency)**

2.454 **V/STOL (vertical and/or short takeoff and landing aircraft)**

2.455 **VTOL (vertical takeoff and landing)**

2.456 **WARNORD (warning order)**

2.457 **Washington, DC (or D.C.).** It is not necessary to spell out the abbreviation in running text.

2.458 **WIA (wounded in action)**

2.459 **WMD (weapons of mass destruction)**

2.460 **WRSK (war readiness/reserve spares kit)**

2.461 **WWW (World Wide Web)**. Shortened form: Web (e.g., Web site, Web page, etc.)

2.462 **XO (executive officer)**

2.463 **zip code or ZIP (zone improvement plan) code; zip (n.); zip-code** (v.). In writing a mailing address, do not use a comma before the ZIP code (or after, if including "USA"): Troy, AL 36081 USA.

2.464 **ZULU (time zone indicator for Universal Time or Greenwich Mean Time)**

3.0 Grammar and Punctuation

3.1 *Grammar*

3.1.1 **active voice**. When the grammatical subject performs the action represented by the verb, the verb is in active voice.

> The congregation sang "Abide with Me."
> Mr. Conrad gave his son a car.
> The police caught the thieves.

See also passive voice (3.1.15).

3.1.2 **aircraft**. Form plurals by adding an *s* (no apostrophe): F-15s, F-22s, F-4Cs, B-52Hs.

3.1.3 **court-martial** (n., v.), **courts-martial** (n., plural)

3.1.4 **dangling modifier**. A verbal phrase at the beginning of a sentence dangles when the word it should modify is not present:

> *Running along the street,* my *nose* felt frozen.

Here, *running along the street* seems to modify *nose*. Correct this problem by adding a word that the verbal phrase can logically modify:

> *Running along the street, I* felt as if my nose were frozen.

3.1.5 **data**. Singular or plural. Choose one, and use it consistently. Be sure that verbs and qualifiers agree with the number that you choose:

> The data is now in, but we have not examined it.
> The data are now in, but we have not examined them.

3.1.6 **first, firstly**. Use *firstly*, *secondly*, and so forth as sentence modifiers; or *first, second*, and so forth. Do not mix the two: *first, secondly.*

3.1.7 **first person**. See I, we (3.1.11).

3.1.8 **he, him, his**. See sexist language (1.49).

3.1.9 **important, importantly**. You may use either word as a sentence modifier. Choose one, and use it consistently.

> More important, the truth will prevail.
> Just as importantly, the truth will prevail.

3.1.10 **it**. Use *it* to refer to inanimate objects and some living things; you may also use this pronoun in impersonal statements and idioms:

> The couple bought a house but did not like it.
>
> The newborn baby kept its eyes shut tightly.
>
> It has been three hours since it began to rain.
>
> We will have to play it by ear.

Using *it* rather than an appropriate personal pronoun or noun can make writing stilted: use *I believe, the Air Force believes*, and so forth, instead of *it is believed*.

3.1.11 **I, we**. You may use *I* or *we* occasionally in the text rather than the formal "the author(s)."

3.1.12 **logistics** (n.). *Logistics* may take either a singular or plural verb. Choose one, and use it consistently.

3.1.13 **media**. *Media* is the plural of *medium*. Use it with a plural verb. Although *media* is used in the singular in references to agencies of mass communications (plural *medias*), that usage is not well established. See also data (3.1.5).

3.1.14 **none**. *None* can be either singular or plural. Choose one, and use it consistently.

> None of those accused was really responsible.
>
> None of those accused were really responsible.

3.1.15 **passive voice**. Passive voice is a verbal construction consisting of a past participle and some form of the verb *be*; all other forms are active.

When the subject of a verb receives the action, the verb is in the passive voice:

> "Abide with Me" was sung by the congregation.
>
> Jimmy was given a car by his father.
>
> The pit was dug fully eight feet deep.
>
> They had been caught.

Characteristics of passive voice:

1. The receiver of the verb's action comes before the verb.
2. The verb has two parts: some form of the verb *be* plus the past participle of a main verb (most of them end in *-en* or *-ed*).

3. If the doer appears at all, it follows the verb and is usually the object of the preposition *by*.

Use passive voice sparingly; otherwise, your writing can become wordy and lack forcefulness. But passive voice has several important uses. In the writer's mind, the object may have more importance than the doer:

The bill was passed without opposition.

The well was drilled in solid rock.

Our house was painted last year.

Use passive voice if you do not want to name the person or thing performing the action. For example:

President Reagan was elected in 1980.

The parts were shipped on 1 June.

Passive voice allows various degrees of emphasis by placing the name of the act or the doer at the end:

Our house is being painted. (Active: They are painting our house.)

Our house was painted by Joe Mead and his brother. (Active: Joe Mead and his brother painted our house.)

"Abide with Me" was sung by the choir. (Active: The choir sang "Abide with Me.")

Since passive voice does not always show the doer, you may forget to include important information. The result may be confusing.

Requests must be approved beforehand. (By whom?)
The commander must approve requests beforehand.

The figures were lost. (By whom?)
We lost the figures.

3.1.16 **that, which.** Clauses introduced by the relative pronouns *that* and *which* are of two kinds: restrictive and nonrestrictive.

A clause is restrictive or defining when the information it provides about something in the main clause is essential to the meaning of the statement. It is generally preceded by the relative pronoun *that*; *which* can also introduce a restrictive clause:

I am looking for the book that (which) I lost yesterday.

A nonrestrictive clause is descriptive, can be set off from the rest of the sentence by commas, must be self-contained, and is introduced only by *which*:

My house, which is old and large, is located on Elm Street.

In some circumstances *that* can be omitted from restrictive clauses:

When it is the object of a verb: the songs (that) we used to sing.

When it is the object of a preposition: the house (that) we made the delivery to.

When it is the complement of some form of the verb *be*: Rascal is not the horse (that) his father was.

When it is technically the subject of the verb *be* but standing in the complement position: We gave him all (that) there was.

Some writers take this option to the extreme by omitting *that* altogether. Oftentimes, however, *that* must be retained for clarity. For example, when a time element follows the verb, the conjunction *that* is always needed to make clear whether the time element applies to the material preceding or following:

Governor Riley announced today that he would sign the income tax bill.

Here, if *that* is omitted, the sentence could mean either that the governor made the announcement today or that he would sign the bill today.

When a sentence with two parallel clauses requires the expression *and that* in the second part, you must retain *that* in the first part of the sentence for parallel construction:

The senator said that she would run next year and that James Corley
would be her campaign manager.

After verbs like *said* or *announced*, you may omit *that* for conciseness: He said (that) he was tired. But if the subject of the clause following the verb can be mistaken for that verb's direct object, *that* must be retained:

He said that a good many things about the project bothered him.

See also which (3.1.22).

3.1.17   **that, which, who, what.** Use *that* to refer to persons, animals, or things; *which* to refer to animals or things; *who, whom,* and *whose* to refer to persons (*but* an argument *whose* point was convincing); and *what* to refer to nonliving things.

3.1.18 **there is, there are**. When *there* is the anticipatory subject, the verb should agree in number with the "real" subject, which follows it: "*There is* a *lesson* to be learned here, and *there are* many more *lessons* to be learned." However, like repeated use of *it is* . . . , repeated use of *there is* . . . and *there are* . . . deprives the sentence of strong subject-verb combinations. See also it (3.1.10).

3.1.19 **this**. Although criticized by some writers, using *this* to refer to the idea conveyed in a preceding sentence is acceptable if the reference is neither confusing nor ambiguous:

> John lost his job. This made his creditors uneasy.

However, do not use *this* when it refers only to some part of an idea or to an antecedent not actually expressed:

> Because of inherited venereal disease, their population remains static. This worries the elders of the tribe. (Venereal disease? Static population? Both?)

> The poet is widely admired, but it is difficult to make a living at this. (Writing poetry, but not expressed in sentence.)

Do not use demonstrative *this* in place of personal pronouns:

> We were much impressed by the tour director. This person (not *this*) is capable and well informed.

3.1.20 **Vietnamese** (n., sing. and pl.; adj.)

3.1.21 **whether**. When this term introduces either a complete or elliptical adverbial clause, use *or not* after *whether*: Whether or not the car was in good condition, he was determined to buy it. In noun clauses, you may use the words *or not* with *whether* for emphasis, but they are not necessary: Whether Tom goes to Birmingham today depends on the weather. When the alternatives are fully expressed, the use of *or not* with *whether* is redundant: Whether he lived inside or outside the city limits was irrelevant. You should repeat *whether* after *or* when the alternatives are long and complex (Whether . . . or whether . . .).

3.1.22 **which**. *Which* can introduce both nonrestrictive and restrictive clauses:

> I read *The Once and Future King*, which is a retelling of Arthurian legend.

> They proposed an operational testing and evaluation method that was based on an approach which evolved from their experiences during the testing of the weapon system.

Which sometimes unambiguously refers to an entire preceding statement rather than to a single word:

> She ignored him, which proved unwise.

Sometimes, however, the antecedent of *which* may be in doubt:

> Some people worry about overeating, which can be unhealthy. (Worrying? Overeating?)

Sometimes it is better to rewrite the sentence:

> Worrying about overeating can be unhealthy.

See also that, which (3.1.16).

3.2.1 **apostrophe**. Form the possessive of singular nouns by adding an apostrophe and an *s*, and the possessive of plural nouns (except for irregular plurals) by adding an apostrophe only: the student's book, the oxen's tails, the libraries' directors. However, if the addition of *'s* to a singular noun causes difficulty in pronunciation, add the apostrophe only: for righteousness' sake. *When the singular form of a noun ends in "s" and the plural form is the same as the singular, form the possessive of both the singular and plural forms by adding an apostrophe only: politics' true meaning, economics' forerunners. The same principle applies when the name of a place or organization is a plural ending in "s" even though the entity is singular: the United States' role in international law, Calloway Gardens' former curator* (*Chicago*, 7.19).

Show joint possession by using the possessive form for the second noun only: Bill and Judy's home. Show individual possession by using the possessive form for both nouns: our dog's and cat's toys. Form expressions of duration in the same way you do possessives: an hour's delay, three weeks' worth, six months' leave of absence.

You can apply the general rule to most proper nouns, including most names ending in sibilants: Burns's poems, Marx's theories, Jefferson Davis's home (but Aristophanes' play), the Rosses' and the Williamses' lands.

To avoid an awkward appearance, use an apostrophe without an s *for the possessive of singular words and names ending in an unpronounced* s (*Chicago, 7.21*): the Marine Corps' motto.

To show possession for compound nouns, add an apostrophe and an *s* to the final word: secretary-treasurer's, mother-in-law's, mothers-in-law's.

To show possession for indefinite pronouns, add an apostrophe and an *s* to the last component of the pronoun: someone's car, somebody else's books.

Do not use apostrophes in plurals of decades identified by century: 1960s, 1980s.

Do not use apostrophes to show plurals of letters and figures unless such punctuation is necessary to avoid confusion: Bs and Cs; 1s, 2s, and 3s; B-52s and F-15s; but A's, a's, i's, and u's.

3.2.2 **brackets**. Use brackets to enclose editorial interpolations within quoted material (to clarify references and make corrections) or in place of parentheses within parentheses.

> "In April [actually July] 1943, Jones published his first novel."

> Gen Charles Horner controlled coalition air assets during the Gulf War (specifically, he was the joint force air and space component commander [JFACC]).

See also sic (1.50).

3.2.3 **bullets**. See display dots (4.5).

3.2.4 **colon**. In a sentence, the presence of a colon indicates a break of the same degree as one indicated by a semicolon. It also signals some sort of relationship between the separated elements. The second element may illustrate or amplify the first:

> Music is more than a collection of notes: it conveys deep feelings and emotions.

Use a colon to introduce a list or a series. If you use *namely, for example*, or *that is* to introduce the list or series, do not use a colon unless the list or series consists of one or more complete clauses:

> The book covered three of the most important writers of the Romantic Period: Byron, Shelley, and Keats.

> The book covered three of the most important writers of the Romantic Period, namely, Byron, Shelley, and Keats.

Use a colon after *as follows* or *the following* to enumerate several items:

> Test scores were as follows: two 95s, two 80s, and one 65.

> The class made the following test scores: two 95s, two 80s, and one 65.

When a colon is used within a sentence, lowercase the first word that follows it unless (1) that word is a proper name, (2) the colon introduces two or more sentences, or (3) the colon introduces speech in a dialogue or extract:

> Beneath the surface, however, is the less tangible question of values: are the old truths true?

> Ed had two must-see attractions on his itinerary: Northwest Florida Alligator Emporium and Crazy Bill's Pink Flamingo Ranch.

> He had two reasons for not attending the awards ceremony: First, he was shy. Second, he had nothing appropriate to wear.

> The umpire heard the fan loud and clear: "You need glasses, you bum!"

Note also that one space, not two, separates the colon from the following text.

Do not use a colon before a series introduced by a verb or preposition:

> *NOT*
> My three immediate goals are: to survive midyear exams, to get to Colorado, and to ski until my legs wear out.
>
> *BUT*
> My three immediate goals are to survive midyear exams. . . .
>
> *NOT*
> His friend accused him of: wiggling in his seat, talking during the lecture, and not remembering what was said.
>
> *BUT*
> His friend accused him of wiggling in his seat. . . .

Place a colon outside quotation marks:

> Will had one objection to the poem "Altarwise by Owl Light at the Halfway House": it was incomprehensible.

See also subtitle (1.54).

3.2.5   **comma**. Use a comma as follows:

- to set off nonrestrictive clauses—those you could omit without changing the meaning of the main clause:

  > Ebeneezer Scrooge, who lived alone, refused to celebrate Christmas.

- after relatively long introductory phrases:

  > After reading the letter from the manufacturer, Mary decided to sue the company.

- before *and* or *or* in a series of three or more elements:

  > Thomas Hobbes said life in the Middle Ages was solitary, poor, nasty, brutish, and short.

- to set off addresses and place-names:

  > The harmless drudge lives at 108 Deerfield Drive, Troy, Alabama, with a full complement of dogs and cats.
  >
  > They moved from Paris, Texas, to Rome, Georgia, in 1987.
  >
  > (Note commas *before* and *after* the name of the state.)

- to separate the independent clauses of a compound sentence:

  > Dr. Lopez criticized the report, and he asked the committee to revise it.

- to separate adjectives that modify the same noun (as a general rule of thumb, if *and* can be substituted for the comma, then the comma is appropriate):

  Most people consider her a generous, outgoing person.

- to separate groups of three digits in numbers of 1,000 or more (except page numbers):

  2,100

  465,230

  5,722,465

- When a comma is needed at the end of material enclosed in quotation marks, parentheses, or brackets, place the comma inside the quotation mark (whether single or double) but outside the closing parenthesis or bracket:

  Tom commented, "The remark 'I mean what I say,'" used by a character in *Alice in Wonderland*, provoked a heated discussion."

  Although the speaker appeared nervous (he stammered quite a bit), he managed to finish his speech.

  When the great ship sailed in 1911 [actually 1912], nobody suspected what lay ahead.

Do not use a comma in the following situations:

- to set off restrictive clauses—those you could not omit without changing the meaning of the main clause:

  The notion that all men are created equal was a radical one.

- after a short introductory phrase:

  By 1865 the Confederacy was clearly doomed.

- to set off the year in military-date style:

  They signed the order on 26 July 1947 in Washington.

- to separate compound predicates in a simple sentence:

  Patsy graduated in May and went to work in June.

- to separate adjectives when the first modifies the combined idea of the second plus the noun:

  The estate is surrounded by an old stone wall.

  The professor was a little old man.

Note that the converse of the rule of thumb for determining whether to use a comma to separate adjectives (see above) applies here: since *and* would not be appropriate either between *old* and *stone* or between *little* and *old*, then no comma is needed.

- to set off *Jr.*, *Sr.*, or a Roman numeral from a name (although commas are no longer necessary with *Jr.* and *Sr.*, you may use them if you wish; if so, place one before and after the abbreviation [choose one style, and use it consistently]; commas never set off Roman numerals when used as part of a name except when the name is inverted, as in an index):

  Harry Connick Jr. plays piano and sings.

  T. Coraghessan Boyle, Sr., is my neighbor.

  Adlai E. Stevenson III

  Stevenson, Adlai E., III. *The Citizen and His Government*. Austin, TX (or Tex.): University of Texas Press, 1984.

See also ZIP code (1.76).

3.2.6 **dash**. The most common dashes are the em dash (sometimes typed as two hyphens) and the en dash (sometimes typed as a hyphen).

Use an em dash or a pair of em dashes to indicate a sudden break or abrupt change in thought:

  My world and the real world—what a contrast!

  He asked—no demanded—that the door be opened.

to sct off interrupting or clarifying elements:

  These are shore deposits—gravel, sand, and clay—but marine deposits underlie them.

to introduce a final statement that summarizes a series of ideas:

  Freedom of speech, freedom of worship, freedom from want, freedom from fear—these are the fundamentals of moral world order.

to set off a word or phrase in the main clause that emphasizes or explains:

  George worked several days on the system—a system that was designed to increase production in the department.

If text set off by a pair of dashes requires a question mark or an exclamation point, place it before the second dash:

  Mr. Incredible's unctuous acquaintance Mr. Blowhard—did he realize how tiresome he was?—excelled at making stupidity a virtue.

Do not use more than one pair of em dashes in a sentence.

The en dash is one-half the length of an em dash and is longer than a hyphen. Use an en dash (signifying *up to and including* or *through*) to connect continuing or inclusive numbers such as dates, time, or reference numbers:

> 1957–63
>
> February–March 1971
>
> pages 12–15

The en dash is also used in place of a hyphen in a compound adjective, one element of which is an open compound or a hyphenated word:

> New York–London flight
>
> Air Force–wide changes
>
> quasi-public–quasi-judicial body

Use an en dash (signifying *to*) to express scores from sporting events, voting results, and travel expressions even though they don't reflect a range of values:

> The Biscuits beat the Lugnuts 12–10 last night.
>
> The delegates to the convention approved the proposal 150–97.
>
> The London–Paris train leaves at two o'clock.

You may also use an en dash to identify a particular university campus:

> The University of Alabama–Huntsville

3.2.7   **ellipses**. Indicate the omission of a word, phrase, line, or paragraph from a quoted passage with ellipsis points, which come in threes; are set on the line like periods; and are separated from each other, from the text, and from any contiguous punctuation by one space.

Use three ellipsis points to indicate an omission in the middle of a quoted sentence: "The nuclear-armed GALOSH ABM interceptor . . . has an inherent ASAT capability against low-altitude satellites." Indicate the omission of the last part of a sentence by a period and three ellipsis points (assuming that more quoted material follows). Leave no space between the period and the preceding word: "The Soviets also have research programs under way on kinetic energy weapons. . . . These programs have been highly successful." Note that *the first word after ellipsis points is capitalized if it begins a grammatically complete sentence, even if it was lowercased in the original* (*Chicago*, 11.55); a space precedes the capitalized word. (Four ellipsis points should be preceded and followed by grammatically complete sentences.) If space so dictates, you may leave the period at the end of a line and begin the next line with three ellipsis points.) *A comma, a colon, a semicolon, a question mark, or an exclamation point may precede or follow three (but never four) ellipsis points* (*Chicago*, 11.58): "What is the major strength of the Soviet space program? . . . This is the question we intended to explore fully." Remember that ellipsis points are seldom used at the beginning or end of a quoted passage.

Indicate the omission of one or more paragraphs in a long block quotation by three ellipsis points following the period at the end of the paragraph preceding the omitted paragraph. If a paragraph in the block quotation—other than the first paragraph—begins with a sentence that does not open the paragraph in the original, it should be preceded by three ellipsis points:

> Such a tremendous increase in capability exceeds their future civil and scientific requirements. The gap between what we perceive to be Soviet launch requirements and launch capabilities is of great concern to us. . . .
>
> . . . This system will expand the current US ICBM field coverage to include US submarine-launched ballistic missiles.

When you replace part of a quoted passage with different wording, enclose the new term(s) with square brackets, but do not use ellipsis points to show that the original wording has been omitted:

> The nuclear-armed GALOSH ABM interceptor deployed around Moscow has an inherent ASAT capability against low-altitude satellites.
>
> The nuclear-armed GALOSH [missile] deployed around Moscow has an inherent ASAT capability against low-altitude satellites.

However, if bracketed material is next to ellipsis points which show that part of a quoted passage has been omitted (and not replaced with different wording), retain the ellipsis points:

> The nuclear-armed GALOSH [missile] . . . has an inherent ASAT capability against low-altitude satellites.

In a run-in quotation, do not use ellipsis points before the first word of the quotation, even if the beginning of the original sentence has been omitted, or after the last word of the quotation, even if the end of the original sentence has been omitted:

> For example, we now know that the Soviets "are currently producing about 50 SL-4/SL-6-type vehicles each year—a rate of nearly one a week."

See also brackets (3.2.2).

3.2.8   **hyphenated compound words**. Compounds are words joined by a hyphen or hyphens, such as *many-sided*, *ill-fated*, and *mother-in-law*. No all-inclusive rule exists for hyphenating compound words. If you are not sure about a particular compound, look it up in the dictionary or *The Chicago Manual of Style's* (15th ed.) "Hyphenation Guide for Compounds, Combining Forms, and Prefixes" (7.90), or refer to "The Writing of Compounds" in *Webster's Third New International Dictionary of the English Language, Unabridged.* The following are a few general principles:

Use a hyphen to prevent ambiguity. For example, *slow moving van* could mean a moving van that is slow (in which case, hyphenating moving van would be acceptable) or a van that is moving slowly: *slow-moving van.* Although adjective compounds traditionally are hyphenated before the noun they modify and are written open after the noun, you may omit the hyphen in all cases if there is no chance of ambiguity or misreading: smoke filled room, red hot iron. This principle holds true even if the compound is hyphenated in the dictionary. Do not hyphenate an adjective compound consisting of an adverb ending in *-ly* plus a participle or an adjective (highly developed organism).

Hyphenate adjective compounds beginning with *well, ill, better, best, little, lesser,* and *least* when they precede the noun, and leave them open after the noun: well-dressed man (*but* the man is well dressed); best-known work (*but* the work is best known); ill-advised action (*but* the action is ill advised). Leave such compounds open when they are modified by an adverb: very well dressed man. If you use quotation marks to enclose an adjective compound that you would normally hyphenate, you may omit the hyphen: "well dressed" man. See also well- (4.2.270).

Measurement compounds are also hyphenated: six-inch-wide board, three-mile limit, 24-gallon tank. If you abbreviate the unit of measure, omit the hyphen: 24 gal. tank.

Compounds consisting of numerals and the word *percent* are left open: 25 percent decrease.

Hyphenate when the second element of a compound is capitalized or is a number: mid-Atlantic tempest, post-1980 developments. Hyphenate when spelling the word solid creates a homonym, as in re-mark (mark again) versus remark (say).

Hyphenate some compounds in which the last letter of the prefix is the same as the first letter of the word following: anti-intellectual, anti-inflammatory.

Use a "suspension" hyphen to carry the force of a modifier to a later noun: second- or third-rate powers; second-, third-, and fourth-grade students.

Some noun compounds are always hyphenated: relative words with *great* and *in-law*, such as great-uncle, great-great-grandmother, sister-in-law; noun plus noun, expressing two different but equally important functions, such as secretary-treasurer; two-word compounds ending in *elect*, such as governor-elect (*but* probate judge elect); some multiple-word compounds including a preposition and describing someone or something, such as jack-of-all-trades (*but* flash in the pan). Some permanent compounds beginning with *vice* are hyphenated, such as vice-chancellor, but not vice admiral or vice president or viceroy. See also vice- (4.2.249).

Do not hyphenate capitalized geographical terms used as adjectives: Southeast Asian country, Mobile Bay cruise. See also compound words (4.2.52); titles of works (4.1.148).

Hyphenate age terms in both adjective and noun forms: a five-year-old child, a five-year-old.

See also word division (1.71).

3.2.9 **omissions**. See ellipses (3.2.7).

3.2.10 **parentheses**. Use parentheses when material inserted in a sentence is so loosely connected with the main thought of the sentence that commas would not be adequate. Such insertions may be explanatory, amplifying, or digressive:

> Another illustration reflects a much more recent instance of a doctrinal notion (table 4).
>
> This manual (issued to all students) covers the fundamental problems.
>
> The funeral for her brother (she misses him terribly) was a sad affair.

If a comma is necessary, place it after the second parenthesis, not before the first. If the parenthetical element within a sentence is itself a sentence, omit the period but retain a question mark or exclamation point:

> As the machine gunner opened fire (it was a .50-caliber gun), all movement ceased.
>
> As the machine gunner opened fire (was it a .50-caliber gun?), all movement ceased.

If parentheses enclose a freestanding sentence, place the period inside the second parenthesis:

> Albert convinced me to go back to college. (I always found his logic irresistible.)

Use parentheses to enclose enumerating letters or numerals (without periods) within a sentence:

> He wanted to (1) consolidate the position, (2) establish contact with guerrillas, and (3) regain control over the inhabitants.

3.2.11 **period**. Place a period at the end of a declarative or imperative sentence. If you use a quotation at the end of a sentence, place the period within the closing quotation mark (double or single). If you use a quotation before the end of a sentence, omit the period or replace it with a comma. To separate sentences, use only one space after a closing quotation mark, as well as after a period or other terminal punctuation (e.g., question mark, exclamation point) (see also colon [3.2.4]). When using parentheses or brackets to enclose a free-standing sentence, place the period inside the final parenthesis or bracket. If the enclosed matter is part of a sentence, place the period outside the final parenthesis or bracket:

> The commander said, "You're only half right."
>
> "One should always say, 'I mean what I say.' "
>
> "I'm sure I say what I mean," said Alice. The Cheshire Cat, however, didn't believe her.
>
> The decision to keep the sentence or drop it is a judgment call. (Writing is hard work precisely because it requires so many judgment calls.)
>
> The driver glanced in his rearview mirror at the passenger (certainly an eccentric fellow).

See also Dr. (doctor) (2.126); Jr. (2.224); lists (1.37); Messrs., Mmes. (2.252); Mr., Mrs., Mme, Ms. (2.269); no. (2.288); parentheses (3.2.10); quotation marks (3.2.14); Sr. (2.384); Truman, Harry S. (1.58).

3.2.12 **possessive**. See apostrophe (3.2.1).

3.2.13 **question mark**. Put a question mark at the end of a direct question that stands alone, as well as one that occurs within a sentence:

> How can I miss you if you won't go away?
>
> How am I going to pass this test? was the question I kept asking myself.
>
> As Mary asked herself, Why am I doing this for him? she glared balefully at John.

Do not put a question mark at the end of an indirect question:

I asked him what he was doing.

How he had managed to fool me was the question no one could answer.

Put a question mark inside quotation marks, parentheses, or brackets only when it is part of the quoted or parenthetical matter:

The colonel asked, "Did you receive our inspection report?"

Did you say, "The base commander wants the report immediately"?

Which of the concepts do you believe to be generally shared (at least by your contemporaries)?

3.2.14 **quotation marks**. Enclose quoted words, phrases, and sentences in double quotation marks. Use single quotation marks to enclose quotations within quotations. Quotations within block quotations require double quotation marks.

Enclose a nickname in quotation marks when it accompanies the full name:

George Herman "Babe" Ruth

Omit the quotation marks when a nickname is used as part of or in place of a personal name:

Stonewall Jackson

the Iron Duke

Enclose a conference title in quotation marks:

"American Writers in the 1930s," a symposium held at the University of Alabama, 15–16 September 1975

but

the 1994 State Conference on Writing across the Curriculum

Use quotation marks to enclose words used in an ironic sense, references to spoken language, and slang terms. Subsequent occurrences of these terms need not include the quotation marks. See also italics (4.4).

The "consultation" could be heard three blocks away.

In Elizabethan dialogue, a change from "you" to "thou" often implies studied insult.

Jacob's grandfather called his Adam's apple his "go fetch it."

Place a comma or a final period within quotation marks, single or double. Put other punctuation marks within quotation marks only if they are part of the quotation. See also period (3.2.11); question mark (3.2.13).

> He said, "I will go."
>
> He asked, "Shall we evacuate the area?"
>
> "I am sure he used the word 'moron.' "

If you place quotation marks around an adjective compound that you would normally hyphenate, you may omit the hyphen: "well dressed" man.

Place a colon outside quotation marks or parentheses:

> There is one problem with Walt Whitman's "O Captain, My Captain": it is doggerel.

You may use quotation marks to refer to a word as a word (see also italics [4.4]):

> The word "boy" has a pejorative sense in some contexts.

Do not enclose words such as *yes, no, where, how,* and *why* in quotation marks when they are used singly, except in direct discourse:

> Ezra always answered yes; he could never say no to a friend.
>
> "Yes," he replied weakly.

Enclose in quotation marks the titles of articles in journals and newspapers; chapter titles; the titles of draft versions of books and other unpublished works; and the titles of short stories, short poems, dissertations, theses, and essays. See also italics (4.4); mottoes (1.38); words as words (4.4.23).

3.2.15 semicolon. Use a semicolon to separate independent clauses not connected by a coordinating conjunction:

> John stayed home for the holidays; he had nowhere else to go.

Use a semicolon (not a comma) before words such as *however, therefore, hence, consequently, moreover, nevertheless,* and so forth, when they connect two independent clauses. (Use a comma after these words.)

> All such missions should remain secondary to the primary mission; however, all commanders of flying Air Force units must prepare to fly such missions with minimum notice.

You may want to use a semicolon with a coordinating conjunction in a compound sentence whose independent clauses are long and contain internal punctuation:

> Ishmael, the narrator, goes to sea, he says, "Whenever it is a damp, drizzly November" in his soul; and Ahab, the captain of the ship, goes to sea because of his obsession to hunt and kill the great albino whale, Moby Dick.

When items in a series are lengthy or contain internal punctuation, separate them by semicolons:

> Mark prepared for the exam by reading the material, which caused him great difficulty; by studying with Tom, who knew less than he did; and by praying, which he did frequently.

> We will need the following supplies: pencils, three boxes; pens, five boxes; paper, four reams; typewriter ribbons, 15; and staples, two boxes.

Place a semicolon outside quotation marks or parentheses:

> Dan's favorite poem is "Stopping by Woods on a Snowy Evening"; he reads it whenever he feels troubled.

> Sam gave his wife a toaster oven for her birthday (he was a very practical fellow); needless to say, she was overwhelmed.

3.2.16 **series of items**. The number of commas separating items in a series should be one fewer than the number of items in the series. Hence, three items in a series should be separated by two commas: planes, boats, and trains. See also comma (3.2.5).

3.2.17 **slash**. *The slash (/)—also known as virgule, solidus, slant, or forward slash, to distinguish it from a backward slash, or backslash (\)—has various distinct uses. . . . A slash most commonly signifies alternatives. . . . Where one or more of the terms separated by slashes is an open compound, a thin space before and after the slash is helpful: he/she, and/or, Hercules/Heracles, World War I / World War II. . . . A slash is used in certain contexts to mean* and: *an MD/Phd student, a Jekyll/Hyde personality. . . . A slash is sometimes used in dates instead of an en dash . . . or even in combination with an en dash, to indicate the last part of one year and the first part of the next: the winter of 1966/67, fiscal years 1991/92–1998/99. . . . In a context where the events of [11 September 2001] are being discussed, 9/11 is quite acceptable. . . . A slash may stand as shorthand for* per, *as in . . . "$450/week" . . . or in certain abbreviations, in lieu of a period, as in "c/o" (in care of). . . . Single and double slashes are used in URLs. No space should precede or follow them. In typeset URLs, line breaks may occur after a slash but not between two slashes.*

(*Chicago*, 6.111–16, 6.119). See also and/or (1.8), dates (1.21), URL (2.425).

3.2.18 year (punctuation with). See dates (4.3.6).

3.2.19 zip code or ZIP (zone improvement plan) code (punctuation with). See 1.76.

4.0 Mechanics

4.1 *Capitalization*

Use as few capital letters as possible, and avoid capitalizing anytime you are in doubt. The following conventions will help you decide whether capital letters are appropriate.

Proper nouns—those that name a particular person, place, or thing—are capitalized. One test of a proper noun is that it does not take a limiting modifier; thus, "*this* [or] *any* [or] *some* 857th Combat Support Group," for example, is not appropriate (since there's only one such group). However, a common noun, which isn't capitalized, can take a limiting modifier, as in "this combat support group" (since it's generic). Because the following examples can take a limiting modifier, they are common nouns and, therefore, are not capitalized:

> base supply
> civil engineer squadron
> military personnel flight
> accounting and finance office

Capitalize civil, military, religious, and professional titles and titles of nobility when they immediately precede someone's name:

> President Bush
> Secretary of Defense Rumsfeld
> Queen Caroline
> Cardinal Richelieu
>
> General Regni
> Sergeant Mann
> Professor Elliott
> Colonel Allen

Capitalize titles associated with more than one person:

> Generals Grant and Lee

Lowercase titles that follow someone's name or that stand alone:

> George W. Bush, president of the United States — the president
> Donald Rumsfeld, secretary of defense — the secretary
> Richard Shelby, senator from Alabama — the senator
> Gen John P. Jumper, Air Force chief of staff — the chief of staff
> Lt Gen John F. Regni, — the commander
>   Air University commander

Lowercase titles used in apposition to a name—no commas (see comma, "restrictive clauses" [3.2.5]):

> Montgomery mayor Bobby Bright
> Air Force general John W. Handy

Capitalize the names of buildings, monuments, and so forth:

the White House	the Eiffel Tower
the Israeli Embassy	the Tomb of the Unknowns

Capitalize the full and (oftentimes) the shortened names of national governmental and military bodies:

US Congress	Congress
Department of Defense	Defense Department, the department
Department of State	State Department, the department
US Air Force	Air Force
US Army	Army
US Marine Corps	Marine Corps, Marines
US Navy	Navy
Montgomery City Council	the city council

Capitalize the full names of boards, committees, organizations, and bureaus:

National Labor Relations Board
Committee on Foreign Affairs
Organization of American States
Bureau of the Census
Veterans Administration

Do not capitalize shortened forms of the full titles for departments, directorates, centers, and similar organizations; the same principle applies to the names of conferences:

Department of Labor	the department
Directorate of Data Processing	the directorate
Center for Strategic Studies	the center
Special Plans Division	the division
Air University Press	the press
Design Branch	the branch
Western Region Writing-Style Conference	the conference

Capitalize the full titles of treaties, laws, acts, bills, amendments, and similar documents, but lowercase their shortened forms:

Intermediate-Range Nuclear Forces (INF) Treaty	the treaty
Conventional Forces in Europe (CFE) Treaty	the treaty
Treaty of Verdun	the treaty
National Labor Relations Act	the labor act, the act
First Amendment (to the US Constitution)	the amendment

Capitalize the full names of judicial bodies; lowercase shortened forms and adjective derivatives:

California Supreme Court, state supreme court
Circuit Court of Calhoun County, county court, circuit court
traffic court, juvenile court

Capitalize the names of national and international organizations, movements, alliances, and members of political parties. The words *party* and *movement* are capitalized when they are part of an organization's name.

The African National Congress party
Bolshevik, Bolshevist, Bolshevik movement, Bolshevism,
 bolshevist (generic), bolshevism (generic)
Communist Party, the party, Communist(s), Communist
 bloc, Communism, communist (generic), communism (generic)
Communist Party USA (CPUSA)
Common Market
Democratic Party, Democrat, democracy, democrat (general
 advocate of democracy)
Eastern bloc
Fascist Party, Fascist(s), fascist (generic), fascism (generic)
Federalist Party, Federalist(s), federalist (generic)
Holy Alliance, the alliance
Marxism-Leninism, Marxist-Leninist, marxism (generic), marxist
 (generic)
right wing, right-winger, leftist, the Right, the Left
Socialist Party, the party, socialism (generic), socialist (generic)

Capitalize the names of generally accepted historical or cultural epochs:

Dark Ages
Jazz Age
Middle Ages
Reformation
Roaring Twenties

but

information age

Capitalize the full titles of armies, navies, air forces, fleets, regiments, battalions, companies, corps, and so forth. Lowercase the words *army*, *navy*, *air force*, and so forth when they are not part of an official title (except when they refer to US forces). Similarly, capitalize the official names of foreign military forces, but lowercase subsequent references to those forces:

Allied armies
Al Quwwat al Jawwiya il Misriya, Egyptian air force, the air force
Army of Northern Virginia

Axis powers
Confederate army (American Civil War)
Continental army (American Revolution)
Eighth Air Force
Fifth Army, the Fifth, the army
1st Battalion, 178th Infantry; the battalion, the 178th
3d [or 3rd] Infantry Division, the division, the infantry
1st Armored Division, the division
III Corps Artillery
French foreign legion
Fuerza Aérea Argentina, Argentinean air force, the air force
Heyl Ha'avir, Israeli air force, the air force
Luftwaffe, the German air force
Nihon Koku Jieitai, Japan air self-defense force, the air self-defense force
the 187th Fighter Group (Air National Guard), the group
People's Liberation Army, Red China's army, the army
Red Army (Russian, World War II), Russian army
Royal Air Force, British air force, the air force
Royal Navy, British navy, the navy
Royal Scots Fusiliers, the fusiliers
Seventh Fleet, the fleet
Twenty-first Air Force
Union army (American Civil War)
United States Air Force, the Air Force
United States Army, the Army, the American Army, the armed Forces
United States Coast Guard, the Coast Guard
United States Marine Corps, the Marine Corps, the US Marines, the Marines, the Corps, Fleet Marine Corps
United States Navy, the Navy
United States Signal Corps, the Signal Corps

Capitalize the full titles of wars but lowercase the words *war* and *battle* when used alone:

American Civil War, the Civil War, the war
American Revolution, the Revolution, the Revolutionary War
Battle of Britain
Battle of the Bulge, the bulge
battle of Bunker Hill, Bunker Hill, the battle
the Blitz
European theater of operations
Falklands War
Gulf War
Korean conflict
Korean War
Operation Overlord

Seven Years' War
Spanish civil war
Tet offensive
Vicksburg campaign
Vietnam War
western front (World War I)
World War I (or 1), the First World War, the war, the two world
  wars
World War II (or 2), the Second World War

Capitalize the names of medals and awards:

Distinguished Flying Cross
Medal of Honor, congressional medal
Purple Heart
Victoria Cross
Croix de Guerre (sometimes lowercased)

Capitalize but don't italicize the designations of make, names of planes, and names of space programs:

Boeing 747   Project Apollo
Concorde   Trident Missile
Nike   U-boat

Do not capitalize or italicize generic types of vessels, aircraft, and so forth:

aircraft carrier
space shuttle
submarine

Capitalize the titles of official documents, instructions, directives, letters, standard forms, and shortened forms of titles, but don't capitalize common nouns that refer to them:

AFMAN 13-220, *Deployment of Airfield Operations*   the manual
AFPAM 11-216, *Air Navigation*   the pamphlet
AFPD 10-1, *Mission Directives*   the policy directive
AFI 63-101, *Acquisition System*   the instruction

Capitalize such words as *empire, state, county,* and so forth, that designate political divisions of the world, when they are part of a proper name. Lowercase these terms when they are not part of a proper name or when they stand alone:

Montgomery County, the county
11th Congressional District, the congressional district, the
  district

Fifth Ward, the ward
Indiana Territory, the territory of Indiana, the territory
New England states
New York City, the city of New York, the city
Roman Empire, the empire
Washington State, the state of Washington
the British colonies

Capitalize all principal words in titles and subheadings. See also titles of works (4.1.148).

Capitalize proper names that designate parts of the world or specific regions:

Central America
central Europe, *but* Central Europe
  (political division of World War I)
the Continent (Europe), the
  European continent
the East, easterner, eastern
  seaboard
eastern Europe, *but* Eastern
  Europe (political division)
Far East
Far West
the Gulf, Persian Gulf region
the North, northerner, Northerner
  (Civil War context)
North Africa, northern Africa

North American continent
North Pole
the South, southerner, Southerner
  (Civil War context)
Southern Hemisphere
South Pacific, southern Pacific
the Southwest (US)
tropic of Cancer
West Coast
western Europe, *but* Western
  Europe (political division)
Western world
Southeast Asia

Lowercase the names of the four seasons unless they are personified; however, capitalize them as part of the date of publication in note references:

spring, summer, fall, winter
In April, Spring sends her showers to pierce the drought of March.
  2. Dr. James H. Toner, "Military OR Ethics," *Air and Space Power Journal* 17, no. 2 (Summer 2003): 80.

Capitalize the names of specific academic courses:

DS 613-Strategic Force Employment
CL 6362-Air Staff Familiarization

Capitalize registered trademark names (see also trademarks [1.57]):

Coca-Cola (*but* cola drink)
Kleenex (*but* tissue)
Band-Aid

Levi's
Ping-Pong (*but* table tennis)
Xerox (*but* xerox [v.])

Capitalize signs, notices, and mottoes in text (see also mottoes [4.1.106]):

> The company had a No Entrance sign at the gate.
> The cry of the French Revolution was Liberty, Equality, and Fraternity.

4.1.1 **academic courses**. Capitalize the names of specific academic courses:

> DS 613-Strategic Force Employment
> CL 6362-Air Staff Familiarization

4.1.2 **active Air Force**

4.1.3 **active duty** (n., adj.)

4.1.4 **acts, amendments, bills, and laws**. Capitalize the full title (formal or popular) of an act or a law, but lowercase all shortened forms: Atomic Energy Act, the act; Sherman Antitrust Law, the antitrust law, the law; Article 6, the article.

A legislative measure is a bill until it is enacted; it then becomes an act or a law. Lowercase the names of bills and proposed constitutional amendments: equal rights amendment (not ratified), food stamp bill.

Capitalize the formal title of an enacted and ratified amendment to the United States Constitution (including the number): the Fifth Amendment, the 18th Amendment. But lowercase informal titles of amendments: the income tax amendment.

4.1.5 **AD (anno Domini)**. Write the abbreviation using either small caps with or without periods or full caps without periods (choose one style, and use it consistently); the abbreviation precedes the year: AD 107. See also BC (before Christ) (2.65, 4.1.26).

4.1.6 **administration**. Capitalize *administration* as part of the proper name of an agency: General Services Administration. Lowercase the term as part of the name of a political organization: Nixon administration.

4.1.7 **agency**. Capitalize *agency* in proper names, but lowercase the shortened form: Federal Security Agency, the agency.

4.1.8 **air base**. Capitalize *air base* when it is part of a proper noun: Kadena Air Base, Japan. Lowercase the shortened form: the air base.

4.1.9 **air force**. Capitalize *air force* when you refer to the US service: United States Air Force, Air Force. Use lowercase letters for an air force in general. Capitalize the term when it is part of the official name of a foreign air force: Royal Air Force. Use lowercase letters for subsequent references: British air force. See also capitalization (4.1).

4.1.10 Air Force base. Capitalize *base* when the full term is part of a proper noun: Maxwell Air Force Base, Alabama. Otherwise, lowercase *base*: the Air Force base.

4.1.11 Air Force One (the president's aircraft)

4.1.12 AirLand Battle

4.1.13 Airman, Airmen (in references to US Air Force personnel)

4.1.14 Air Staff

4.1.15 allied, allies. Capitalize *allied* or *allies* in the context of World War I and World War II.

4.1.16 a.m. (ante meridiem [before noon]). Either write the abbreviation in lowercase with periods or set it in small caps without periods (choose one style, and use it consistently). See also p.m. (post meridiem [after noon]) (4.1.118).

4.1.17 amendments. See acts, amendments, bills, and laws (4.1.4).

4.1.18 appendix. Capitalize *appendix* as a document title: Appendix A, Appendix B, Appendix C. Lowercase the term in textual references (see appendix A). If you wish to include a document such as an Air Force instruction as an appendix to your study, reproduce that document verbatim.

4.1.19 armed forces

4.1.20 army. Capitalize *army* when you refer to the US service: United States Army, Army. Lowercase the term when you refer to an army in general. Capitalize *army* when it is part of the official name of a foreign army: Red Army. Use lowercase letters for subsequent references: Russian army. See also capitalization (4.1).

4.1.21 article (part of a document). See acts, amendments, bills, and laws (4.1.4).

4.1.22 **associate's degree**. Capitalize the name of the degree (Associate of Arts, Associate of Science) when it follows someone's name (John Smith, Associate of Arts). Lowercase the term when referring to the degree in general terms (John Smith has an associate of arts degree). See also academic degrees and titles (2.6); bachelor's degree (4.1.23); doctorate (4.1.55); master's degree (4.1.97).

4.1.23 **bachelor's degree**. Capitalize the name of the degree (Bachelor of Arts, Bachelor of Science) when it follows someone's name (John Smith, Bachelor of Arts). Lowercase the term when referring to the degree in general terms (John Smith has a bachelor of arts degree). See also academic degrees and titles (2.6); associate's degree (4.1.22); doctorate (4.1.55); master's degree (4.1.97).

4.1.24 **battalion**. Capitalize *battalion* in proper names: 3d [or 3rd] Battalion, 10th Battalion.

4.1.25 **battle**. Capitalize *battle* in proper names (you may lowercase the term to indicate the location where the battle took place): Battle of the Bulge, battle of Bunker Hill.

4.1.25.1 Battlefield Airman/Airmen

4.1.26 **BC (before Christ)**. Write the abbreviation using either small caps with or without periods or full caps without periods (choose one style, and use it consistently); the abbreviation follows the year: 240 BC. See also AD (anno Domini) (2.9, 4.1.5).

4.1.27 **Berlin airlift**

4.1.28 **Berlin Wall**

4.1.29 **bills (congressional)**. See acts, amendments, bills, and laws (4.1.4).

4.1.30 **black (people)** (n., adj.). You may either capitalize or lowercase this term; choose one style, and use it consistently. See also white (people) (4.1.158).

4.1.31 **board**. Capitalize *board* when it is part of a proper name: National Labor Relations Board. Lowercase it in generic references: the board.

4.1.32 **Bosnian crisis**

4.1.33 **building names**. Capitalize the names of governmental buildings, churches, office buildings, hotels, and specially designated rooms:

the Capitol (state or national), Criminal Courts Building, First Presbyterian Church, Empire State Building, Oak Room.

4.1.34 **bureau**. Capitalize *bureau* when it is part of a proper name but not in reference to a newspaper's news bureau: Bureau of Indian Affairs, Newspaper Advertising Bureau, Washington bureau of the *New York Times*.

4.1.35 **chief of staff**. See capitalization (4.1).

4.1.36 **civil service**

4.1.37 **coalition forces**

4.1.38 **cold war or Cold War**. Lowercase *cold war* in references to an ideological conflict in general; uppercase the term in references to the ideological conflict between the United States and the Soviet Union.

4.1.39 **committee**. See congressional committees and subcommittees (4.1.46).

4.1.40 **communism**. See capitalization (4.1).

4.1.41 **communist**. See capitalization (4.1).

4.1.42 **Communist bloc**. See capitalization (4.1).

4.1.43 **Communist Party**. See capitalization (4.1).

4.1.44 **Congress**. Capitalize this term when referring to the US Congress.

4.1.45 **congressional**. Lowercase *congressional* except when it is part of a particular title or office: *Congressional Record*, Congressional Budget Office, congressional district.

4.1.46 **congressional committees and subcommittees**. Capitalize *committee* or *subcommittee* when either is part of a full title: Committee on Foreign Affairs, the committee; Subcommittee on Energy and the Environment, the subcommittee.

4.1.47 **congressman, congresswoman**. Lowercase *congressman* and *congresswoman* except when they precede a person's name. Capitalize *senator* and *representative* when they precede a person's name:

Congresswoman Lowey, the congresswoman from New York; Senator Shelby, the senator from Alabama. See also abbreviations (2.0).

4.1.48 **constitutional amendments**. Capitalize the full titles of amendments to the US Constitution: Fifth Amendment, 18th Amendment, the amendment. See also acts, amendments, bills, and laws (4.1.4).

4.1.49 **courses, academic**. See capitalization (4.1).

4.1.50 **Cuban missile crisis**

4.1.51 **Democratic Party, Democrat(s) (member[s] of the party), democracy**. See also capitalization (4.1).

4.1.52 **department**. See capitalization (4.1).

4.1.53 **directions (north, south, east, west, north-northwest [NNW], north-northeast [NNE], south-southwest [SSW], south-southeast [SSE])**. See also capitalization (4.1).

4.1.54 **director, directorate**. See capitalization (4.1).

4.1.55 **doctorate**. Capitalize the name of the degree (Doctor of Philosophy, Doctor of Education) when it follows someone's name (John Smith, Doctor of Philosophy). Lowercase the term when referring to the degree in general terms (John Smith has a doctorate). See also academic degrees and titles (2.6); associate's degree (4.1.22); bachelor's degree (4.1.23); master's degree (4.1.97).

4.1.56 **earth**. *In nontechnical writing, do not capitalize "earth" (in the sense of our planet) when preceded by "the" or in such idioms as "down to earth." When the term is used as the proper name of our planet, especially in context with other planets, capitalize it, usually omitting "the" (Chicago, 8.149).*

> *Some still believe the earth is flat.*
> *Where on earth have you been?*
> *The astronauts have successfully returned to Earth.*

The words "sun" and "moon" are usually lowercased in nontechnical text and always lowercased in the plural (Chicago, 8.150).

> *The moon circles the earth as the earth circles the sun.*
> *Jupiter has several moons.*

4.1.57 Earth station

4.1.58 e-mail (n., sing. and pl.).

4.1.59 e-mail (v.)

4.1.60 e-mailer (n.)

4.1.61 empire. See capitalization (4.1).

4.1.62 exercises. Capitalize only the initial letter(s) of the name of the exercise unless the name is an acronym: Desert Strike, REFORGER (return of forces to Germany). See also operations, names of (4.1.112).

4.1.63 federal, federal government

4.1.64 floor leader. Lowercase *floor leader*, whether preceding or following the name:

> He consulted floor leader Hugh L. Brown, a Republican.
>
> Rep. Hugh L. Brown, the Republican floor leader, was available for questions.

4.1.65 foreign military services. See capitalization (4.1).

4.1.66 fort. Spell out and capitalize *fort* when it is part of a proper name: Fort Hood.

4.1.67 free world or Free World

4.1.68 führer or fuehrer

4.1.69 general (military rank). See abbreviations (2.0); capitalization (4.1); military titles and offices (2.258).

4.1.70 Geneva convention(s)

4.1.71 g-force

4.1.72 global war on terrorism (GWOT)

4.1.73 government, federal government, US government

4.1.74 **group**. Capitalize *group* when it is part of a proper name: 42d [or 42nd] Medical Group, the group.

4.1.75 **G suit**

4.1.76 **Gulf War**. See also capitalization (4.1); Persian Gulf War (4.1.116).

4.1.77 **headquarters**. Spell out and capitalize *headquarters* when referring to Air Force headquarters and headquarters of major commands: Headquarters USAF, Headquarters ACC, *but* the headquarters.

4.1.78 **highway**. Capitalize *highway* in proper names, but lowercase the shortened form: Alcan Highway, the highway. Use Arabic numerals to designate state, federal, and interstate highways: Interstate 85, Alabama 41.

4.1.79 **Ho Chi Minh Trail**

4.1.80 **house**. Capitalize *house* when referring to the House of Representatives, in full or shortened form: the House. Lowercase in other contexts: the lower house of Congress.

4.1.81 **information age**

4.1.82 **international date line**

4.1.83 **Internet (the global network of computers)**

4.1.84 **iron curtain**. The term *iron curtain* is often capitalized when it refers to the political, military, and ideological barrier that isolated an area under control of the former Soviet Union.

4.1.85 **jeep**. Lowercase *jeep* when referring to a military vehicle. Capitalize when referring to the trademark of the civilian vehicle.

4.1.86 **joint doctrine**

4.1.87 **Joint Staff**. The staff under the chairman of the Joint Chiefs of Staff.

4.1.88 **journals**. Capitalize all main words of the title of a journal, and italicize both the full title and its abbreviation: *Air and Space Power Journal, ASPJ*. See also italics (4.4); titles of works (4.1.148).

4.1.89 **judicial branch**. See capitalization (4.1).

4.1.90 **Korean conflict**

4.1.91 **Korean War**

4.1.92 **laws**. See acts, amendments, bills, and laws (4.1.4).

4.1.93 **legislative bodies, legislative branch**. See capitalization (4.1).

4.1.94 **localities and regions**. Capitalize the popular names of specific localities and regions: East Side, Sun Belt, Twin Cities. See also capitalization (4.1).

4.1.95 **Marine Corps, Marine(s), marine**. Capitalize *Marine(s)* as a synonym for the US Marine Corps: Jim enlisted in the Marines; a Marine landing; *but* three marines, a company of marines. Shortened title: Marine Corps, the Corps. As a guide to capitalization, apply the following test: If the word *soldier* or *soldiers* would fit logically in place of *marine* or *marines*, use *m*. If *Army*, *Navy*, or *Air Force* can be substituted logically for *Marines*, use *M*.

4.1.96 **Marshall Plan, the plan**

4.1.97 **master's degree**. Capitalize the name of the degree (Master of Arts, Master of Science) when it follows someone's name (John Smith, Master of Arts). Lowercase the term when referring to the degree in general terms (John Smith has a master of arts degree). See also academic degrees and titles (2.6); MAAS (2.245.1); MMOAS (2.261.1); MSS (2.270.1); associate's degree (4.1.22); bachelor's degree (4.1.23); doctorate (4.1.55).

4.1.98 **medals**. Capitalize names of specific medals and awards:

> Medal of Honor; congressional medal
> Distinguished Flying Cross
> Legion of Merit

See also capitalization (4.1).

4.1.99 **Middle Ages**

4.1.100 **MiG(s)**. Capital *M*, lowercase *i*, capital *G*. Soviet aircraft developed by the design bureau of Gen Artem *Mi*koyan and Gen Mikhail *G*urevich.

4.1.101 **military establishment**

4.1.102 **military-industrial complex**

4.1.103 **military terms**. Capitalize proper names of armies, navies, air forces, fleets, regiments, battalions, companies, corps, and so forth. Lowercase the words *army*, *navy*, *air force*, and so forth, standing alone or when they are not part of a proper name (except when they refer to US forces):

> When questioned about a separate air force, the general saw it as a matter for the Army to decide.

See also capitalization (4.1).

4.1.104 **military titles and offices**. See 2.258.

4.1.105 **moon**. See earth (4.1.56).

4.1.106 **mottoes**. Enclose mottoes and similar expressions in quotation marks, capitalize them as if they were titles, or capitalize the first word only:

> "A penny saved is a penny earned" was his favorite maxim.
> The flag bore the motto Don't Tread on Me.
> He was fond of the motto All for one and one for all.

4.1.107 **naval forces**. Lowercase *naval forces*, but use *Navy forces* in the context of the US Navy.

4.1.108 **naval station**. Capitalize *naval station* only in proper names: Norfolk Naval Station, the naval station, the station. Use *Navy station* to refer to a US Navy installation.

4.1.109 **Navy**. Capitalize *Navy* when referring to the US service. For foreign naval forces, see capitalization (4.1).

4.1.110 **nuclear triad**

4.1.111 **officials, government**. See capitalization (4.1).

4.1.112 **operations, names of**. Write the names of operations with initial capital letters: Operation Haylift, Operation Torch, Operation Crossroad, Operations Desert Shield and Desert Storm, Operation Iraqi Freedom.

4.1.113 **organizations**. See capitalization (4.1).

4.1.114 **panzer (German tank)**

4.1.115   **party (political)**. See capitalization (4.1).

4.1.116   **Persian Gulf War**. See also capitalization (4.1); Gulf War (4.1.76).

4.1.117   **plans**. Capitalize the names of military plans.

> Air War Plans Division, Plan 1 (AWPD-1), Munitions Requirements of the Army Air Forces

4.1.118   **p.m. (post meridiem [after noon])**. Either write the abbreviation in lowercase with periods or set it in small caps without periods (choose one style, and use it consistently). See also a.m. (ante meridiem [before noon]) (4.1.16).

4.1.119   **president**. Capitalize *president* only when the term precedes a person's name; otherwise, lowercase it. Abbreviate the term when it precedes a full name; spell it out when it precedes a surname only (Pres. John F. Kennedy, President Kennedy, the president). See also capitalization (4.1); abbreviations (2.0).

4.1.120   **RAND Corporation or RAND**

4.1.121   **regiment**. 2d [or 2nd] Armored Cavalry Regiment, the regiment. See also capitalization (4.1); military units (4.3.17).

4.1.122   **regions of the world**. See capitalization (4.1).

4.1.123   **regular**. Capitalize *regular* when it is part of the name of a component: Regular Air Force, Regular Army.

4.1.124   **Republican Party, Republican(s) (member[s] of the party)**. See also capitalization (4.1).

4.1.125   **Reserve(s)**. Capitalize *Reserve(s)* if the term is part of the name of a component: Air Force Reserve, Ready Reserve, Standby Reserve. Capitalize it as a synonym for Air Force Reserve: the Reserve. *But* write reserve component, the reserve officer, the reservist(s) (all generic, service unspecified). As a guide to capitalization, apply the following test: if *Air Force Reserve* can be logically substituted for *reserve*, use R. The same rule applies to other military services.

4.1.126   **seasons**. Do not capitalize the four seasons unless they are personified: spring, summer, fall, winter. Capitalize them in publication dates in endnotes for journal references: (Fall 2003). See also capitalization (4.1).

4.1.127 **security classification**. Capitalize only the initial letter of a term indicating a specific security classification: Secret, Confidential.

4.1.128 **Senate**. Capitalize this term in references to the US Senate.

4.1.129 **senator**. Capitalize *senator* when it precedes someone's name (do not abbreviate it before a full name); lowercase the term when it follows a personal name or is used alone in place of a name: Senator Richard Shelby; Senator Shelby; Richard Shelby, Republican senator from Alabama; the senator from Alabama. See also abbreviations (2.0); capitalization (4.1).

4.1.130 **service**. Lowercase *service* in references to one of a nation's military forces (e.g., an army or navy).

4.1.131 **show of force**

4.1.132 **Signal Corps, the corps**

4.1.133 **Smithsonian Institution**

4.1.134 **Socialist Party, Socialist (member of the party), socialism, socialist (advocate of socialism)**. See capitalization (4.1).

4.1.135 **South**. Capitalize this term in references to a specific geographical region. See also capitalization (4.1).

4.1.136 **space programs**. Capitalize but do not italicize the names of space programs: Project Apollo.

4.1.137 **space shuttle**

4.1.138 **Speaker of the House of Representatives, the Speaker of the House, the Speaker**. Capitalize *Speaker* to avoid ambiguity.

4.1.139 **Spetsnaz**

4.1.140 **Sputnik**. Capitalize this term; italicize when it is part of the name of a specific satellite: *Sputnik II*.

4.1.141 **squadron**. Capitalize *squadron* in references to a numbered unit, but lowercase it when used alone: 732d [or 732nd] Bomber Squadron, the squadron.

4.1.142 **standby** (n., adj.). Capitalize *standby* in references to the Air Force Reserve: Standby Reserve. See also Reserve(s) (4.1.125).

4.1.143 **stealth bomber, stealth technology**

4.1.144 **sun**. See earth (4.1.56).

4.1.145 **Supreme Court (of the United States)**. Shortened form: the Court. See also capitalization (4.1).

4.1.146 **theater, theatre**. Shortened form of *theater of operations* or *theater of war*. Lowercase, as in European theater. Either spelling is standard; choose one, and use it consistently.

4.1.147 **third world or Third World** (n., adj.)

4.1.148 **titles of works**. Capitalize the first and last words and all nouns, pronouns, adjectives, verbs, adverbs, and subordinating conjunctions in titles and subheadings. Lowercase articles *(the, a, an)*, coordinating conjunctions *(and, but, or, for, nor, yet, so)*, and prepositions, unless they are the first or last words of the title or subtitle. Lowercase the *to* in infinitives.

> The Problem with Our Airpower Doctrine

Always capitalize the first element of a hyphenated compound word in a title; capitalize the other elements unless they are articles, prepositions, or coordinating conjunctions:

> Eighteenth-Century Fiction
> Over-the-Hill Gang
> Fly-by-Night Businesses

Do not capitalize the second element of a hyphenated prefix unless it is a proper noun or proper adjective:

> Anti-inflationary Guidelines
> Non-Christian Religions

Do not capitalize the second element of a hyphenated, spelled-out number:

> Lolita's Twenty-first Birthday

Capitalize the final element of a hyphenated compound at the end of a title, unless it is a hyphenated prefix:

Avoiding a Run-In
Haven of Anti-intellectualism

See also italics (2.0).

4.1.149 **treaties, pacts, and plans**. See capitalization (4.1).

4.1.150 **Vietnam War**

4.1.151 **wars**. Capitalize full titles of wars, but lowercase the shortened form: Spanish-American War, the war; Korean War, the war; Vietnam War, the war.

4.1.152 **Warsaw Pact, Warsaw Pact nations**

4.1.153 **Web, Web site, Web-site** (adj). See also WWW (World Wide Web) (2.461).

4.1.154 **West(ern)**. Capitalize terms that include *West(ern)* if they are considered proper names; lowercase such terms if they are not considered proper names or if they are merely directional: Western world, the West, Midwest (US), Far West, but western, far western, western Pacific Ocean. See also capitalization (4.1).

4.1.155 **western front (World War I)**

4.1.156 **Western Hemisphere**

4.1.157 **white paper**. Lowercase *white paper* unless it is part of a title:

The State Department summarized its findings in a white paper on terrorism.

The State Department released its findings in a report, "A White Paper on Terrorism."

4.1.158 **white (people)**. (n., adj.). You may either capitalize or lowercase this term; choose one style, and use it consistently. See also black (people) (4.1.30).

4.1.159 **wing**. Capitalize *wing* when it is part of a proper name: 42d [or 42nd] Air Base Wing, *but* the wing.

4.1.160   **work order**. Lowercase *work order* when it is used generically. Capitalize the term when it is part of a title (e.g., Minor Maintenance Work Order [AF Form 1827]).

4.1.161   **Wright brothers**

4.1.162   **Xerox, xerox** (v.). See also 1.74.

4.1.163   **zip code or ZIP (zone improvement plan) code**. See also 1.76.

 Spelling and Word Formation

This style guide uses *Webster's Third New International Dictionary of the English Language, Unabridged* and the 11th edition of *Merriam-Webster's Collegiate Dictionary* as authoritative sources for the spelling of common words. These dictionaries often identify variations in spelling that are considered standard usage (e.g., toward *or* towards; adviser *also* advisor; flyer *variant of* flier). Either spelling is acceptable. Select the one you prefer, and use it consistently throughout a particular piece of writing. For the spelling of place-names, refer to such authoritative sources as the *Columbia Gazetteer of North America, The Times Atlas of the World, Merriam-Webster's Geographical Dictionary*, and the section "Geographical Names" in *Merriam-Webster's Collegiate Dictionary*, 11th edition. Note that the noun forms listed below can also be used attributively (e.g., African-American population).

4.2.1 African-American (n.)

4.2.2 Afro-American (n.)

4.2.3 aiming point (n.)

4.2.4 air base (n.)

4.2.5 air chief marshal (n.)

4.2.6 aircrew (n.)

4.2.7 airdrop (n.)

4.2.8 air-drop (v.)

4.2.9 air-droppable (adj.)

4.2.10 airfield (n.)

4.2.11 airframe (n.)

4.2.12 airhead (n.)

4.2.13 airland (v.)

4.2.14 AirLand Battle

4.2.15 air lane (n.)

4.2.16 airlift (n., v.)

4.2.17 Airman (n.)

4.2.18 air marshal (n.)

4.2.19 air-minded (adj.)

4.2.20 air-mindedness (n.)

4.2.21 airmobile (adj.)

4.2.22 airpower (n.). But land power, sea power, space power.

4.2.23 airspace (n.)

4.2.24 airspeed (n.)

4.2.25 air strike (n.)

4.2.26 airstrip (n.)

4.2.27 air vice-marshal (n.)

4.2.28 airworthiness (n.)

4.2.29 airworthy (adj.)

4.2.30 al-Qaeda

4.2.31 anti-. Words formed with the prefix *anti* are usually solid: antiaircraft, antisubmarine. Exceptions include capitalized words (anti-Semitic), repeated vowels (anti-inflammatory), and misleading or difficult-to-read forms (anti-utopia). See also compound words (4.2.52).

4.2.32 Ba'ath Party

4.2.33 battlefield (n.)

4.2.34 battlefront (n.)

4.2.35 battleground (n.)

4.2.36 battle line (n.)

4.2.37 battlespace (n.)

4.2.38 beddown (n.)

4.2.39 bed down (v.)

4.2.40 bin Laden, Osama

4.2.41 biplane (n.)

4.2.42 Brookings Institution

4.2.43 buildup (n.)

4.2.44 build up (v.)

4.2.45 by-product (n.)

4.2.46 call sign (n.)

4.2.47 cease-fire (n.)

4.2.48 choke point (n.)

4.2.49 citizen-soldier (n.)

4.2.50 code name (n.)

4.2.51 code-name (v.)

4.2.52 compound words. There are three types of compound words: open (air brake), solid (aircrew), and hyphenated (air-dry). Compounds are either permanent (found in the dictionary) or temporary (not found in the dictionary). Use the dictionary's spelling of permanent compounds. For help in the spelling of compounds, refer to the "Hyphenation Guide for Compounds, Combining Forms, and Prefixes" (7.90) in *The Chicago Manual of Style*, 15th edition. When in doubt, use open spelling for a temporary compound (e.g., war fighter). See also "The Writing of Compounds" in *Webster's Third New International Dictionary of the English Language, Unabridged.*

Words formed with prefixes like *non-*, *pre-*, and *re-* are usually solid: nonnuclear, prearrange, reenlist.

Words with the suffix *-like* are often used to form new compounds and are generally solid: childlike, businesslike, lifelike; *but* bull-like, Faulkner-like.

Words combined with the suffix *-fold* are solid unless they are formed with numerals: threefold, multifold, 20-fold.

A few noun compounds are always open: those beginning with relationship words, such as Mother Nature, fellow traveler, sister ship, parent company, and most compounds ending with *general*, such as attorney general, adjutant general, and comptroller general (*but* governor-general).

Adjective compounds consisting of adverbs ending in *-ly* plus participles or adjectives are left open: poorly written story, rapidly developing area. Compounds formed from unhyphenated proper names are left open: Methodist Episcopal Church, Southeast Asian country. Chemical names are open: carbon monoxide poisoning, hydrochloric acid bottle. Words naming colors are open: sea green gown, grayish blue car.

Combining forms (e.g., electrocardiogram, socioeconomic, politico-scientific, practico-inert, network-centric) are usually closed if permanent, hyphenated if temporary (Chicago, 7.90). See also hyphenated compound words (3.2.8) and "Words Formed with Prefixes," in "Hyphenation Guide for Compounds, Combining Forms, and Prefixes," in *The Chicago Manual of Style*, 15th edition, pp. 306–8.

4.2.53 **copilot** (n.)

4.2.54 **cost-effective** (adj.)

4.2.55 **cost-effectiveness** (n.)

4.2.56 **counter-**. Compound words with the prefix *counter* are usually solid: counterair, countermeasure, counterblow, counterclockwise. See also compound words (4.2.52).

4.2.57 **countries**. Spell out the names of countries in text. See also abbreviations (2.0); United States (1.59); US (United States) (2.426); USSR (Union of Soviet Socialist Republics) (2.444).

4.2.58 **court-martial** (n., v.), **courts-martial** (n., plural)

4.2.59 **coworker** (n.)

4.2.60   **crew member** (n.)

4.2.61   **cross-train** (v.)

4.2.62   **cyberspace** (n.)

4.2.63   **database** (n., v.)

4.2.64   **data link** (n.)

4.2.65   **data-link** (v., adj.)

4.2.66   **daytime** (n.)

4.2.67   **D-day** (n., adj.)

4.2.68   **decision maker** (n.)

4.2.69   **decision making** (n.)

4.2.70   **decision-making** (adj.)

4.2.71   **de-emphasize** (v.)

4.2.72   **dive-bomb** (v.)

4.2.73   **dive-bomber** (n.)

4.2.74   **downsize** (v.)

4.2.75   **drawdown** (n.)

4.2.76   **draw down** (v.)

4.2.77   **e-mail** (n., sing. and pl.)

4.2.78   **e-mail** (v.)

4.2.79   **e-mailer** (n.)

4.2.80   **endgame** (n.)

4.2.81   **endnotes**. See notes (5.1).

4.2.82   **end state** (n.)

4.2.83   **end-state** (adj.)

4.2.84   **en masse** (adv.)

4.2.85   **en route** (adv., adj.)

4.2.86   **ensure**. To make sure or certain, guarantee. See also insure (4.2.132).

4.2.87   **fact finder** (n.)

4.2.88   **fact-finding** (n., adj.)

4.2.89   **fait accompli** (n. sing.), **faits accomplis** (n. pl.) (a thing accomplished and presumably irreversible).

4.2.90   **feedback** (n.)

4.2.91   **field marshal** (n.)

4.2.92   **field test** (n.)

4.2.93   **field-test** (v.)

4.2.94   **fighter-bomber** (n.)

4.2.95   **fighter pilot** (n.)

4.2.96   **firearm** (n.)

4.2.97   **firebomb** (n., v.)

4.2.98   **firepower** (n.)

4.2.99   **firsthand** (adj., adv.)

4.2.100   **flight crew** (n.)

4.2.101   **flight line** (n.)

4.2.102   **flight-line** (adj.)

4.2.103   **flight path** (n.)

4.2.104   **flight suit** (n.)

4.2.105   **flight-test** (v.)

4.2.106   **followership** (n.)

4.2.107   **follow-on** (n.)

4.2.108   **follow-up** (n.)

4.2.109   **follow up** (v.)

4.2.110   **footnote** (n.) See notes (5.1).

4.2.111   **foreword** (n.) See also foreword (1.28).

4.2.112   **front line** (n.)

4.2.113   **frontline** (adj.)

4.2.114   **führer or fuehrer**

4.2.115   **full time** (n.)

4.2.116   **full-time** (adj., adv.)

4.2.117   **Gadhafi, Mu'ammar**

4.2.118   **geo-**. Most compounds with the prefix *geo* are solid: geoeconomics, geomagnetic, geonavigation, geopolitics.

4.2.119   **g-force** (n.)

4.2.120   **G suit** (n.)

4.2.121   **half-**. Most adjective compounds with the prefix *half* are hyphenated; a few are closed: half-blooded, half-cocked, half-witted, halfhearted, halfway. See also compound words (4.2.52); hyphenated compound words (3.2.8).

4.2.122   **half century** (n.)

4.2.123   **high-**. Most adjective compounds with the prefix *high* are hyphenated before the noun: high-level meeting. After the noun, write them open (but hyphenate after the noun if doing so will prevent ambiguity). Some compounds with this prefix are closed: highbrow, highfalutin, highland. See also compound words (4.2.52); hyphenated compound words (3.2.8).

4.2.124 **home page** (n.)

4.2.125 **Hussein, Saddam**

4.2.126 **ill-**. See hyphenated compound words (3.2.8).

4.2.127 **inbrief** (v.)

4.2.128 **inbriefing** (n., v.)

4.2.129 **in depth** (adv.)

4.2.130 **in-depth** (adj.)

4.2.131 **in-process** (v.)

4.2.132 **insure**. This term is often synonymous with *ensure* (i.e., to make certain by taking necessary measures and precautions). *Insure* also carries the distinctive sense of providing or obtaining insurance. See also ensure (4.2.86).

4.2.133 **inter-**. The prefix *inter* nearly always occurs in solid compounds: interrelated, interaction, international. Add a hyphen when the second element is capitalized: inter-American. See also compound words (4.2.52); hyphenated compound words (3.2.8).

4.2.134 **in-theater** (adj., adv.)

4.2.135 **-keeper**. Compound words with the suffix *keeper* are usually written solid: bookkeeper, scorekeeper, timekeeper, hotelkeeper; *but* tollgate keeper. See also compound words (4.2.52).

4.2.136 **landmass** (n.)

4.2.137 **land power** (n.)

4.2.138 **log in** (v.)

4.2.139 **log-in** (n.)

4.2.140 **logistic or logistical** (adj.)

4.2.141   **log off** (v.)

4.2.142   **log-off** (n.)

4.2.143   **log on** (v.)

4.2.144   **log-on** (n.)

4.2.145   **long term** (n.)

4.2.146   **long-term** (adj.)

4.2.147   **longtime** (adj.)

4.2.148   **man-**. The prefix *man* occurs in solid, hyphenated, and open compound words: mankind, man-hour(s), man jack. See also compound words (4.2.52); hyphenated compound words (3.2.8); sexist language (1.49); work hour(s) (4.2.281).

4.2.149   **man-hour(s)** (n.). See also sexist sexist language (1.49); work hour(s) (4.2.281).

4.2.150   **material, matériel (or materiel)** (n.) *Material* refers to any matter or substance from which something is made. *Materiel* refers more specifically to apparatus or equipment (e.g., military supplies).

4.2.151   **microcomputer** (n.)

4.2.152   **mid-**. Adjective compounds with the prefix *mid* are usually solid unless the second element begins with a capital letter: midair collision, mid-Atlantic tempest. Noun compounds with this prefix are usually solid; if the second word is a proper noun, the compound may be either open or hyphenated: midsummer, mid Atlantic, mid-Victorian, mid-1944 (all of the following are acceptable: mid-to late 1944, mid-to-late 1944, mid to late 1944). See also compound words (4.2.52); hyphenated compound words (3.2.8).

4.2.153   **militia** (sing.), **militias** (pl.)

4.2.154   **Milošević, Slobodan**

4.2.155   **mind-set** (n.)

4.2.156   **minelayer** (n.)

4.2.157 **mine laying** (n.)

4.2.158 **mine-laying** (adj.)

4.2.159 **minesweeper** (n.)

4.2.160 **minesweeping** (n., v.)

4.2.161 **missileman** (n.)

4.2.162 **multi-**. Words with the prefix *multi* are usually solid: multibreak, multicylinder, multiengine. See also compound words (4.2.52).

4.2.163 **must-read** (n.)

4.2.164 **nation-state** (n.)

4.2.165 **near real time** (n.)

4.2.166 **near-real-time** (adj.)

4.2.167 **near term** (n.)

4.2.168 **near-term** (adj.)

4.2.168.1 **network-centric** (adj.) See also compound words (4.2.52).

4.2.169 **nighttime** (n.)

4.2.170 **non-**. Words with the prefix *non* are usually solid: nonviolent, nonoperating, nonnegotiable, nonparty. *But* non-English-speaking world. See also compound words (4.2.52).

4.2.171 **off-line** (adj., adv.)

4.2.172 **off-load** (v.)

4.2.173 **onboard** (adj.). An onboard computer.

4.2.174 **on board** (adv.). Aboard. He is on board the ship.

4.2.175 **ongoing** (adj.)

4.2.176 **online** (adj., adv.)

4.2.177 **onload** (v.)

4.2.178   **on-station** (adj.)

4.2.179   **on station** (adv.)

4.2.180   **outbrief** (v.)

4.2.181   **outbriefing** (n., v.)

4.2.182   **out-process** (v.)

4.2.183   **over-**. Compound words with the prefix *over* are usually solid: overage, overproduction, overeager, override. See also compound words (4.2.52).

4.2.184   **part-time** (adj., adv.)

4.2.185   **part-timer** (n.)

4.2.186   **peacekeeper** (n.)

4.2.187   **peacekeeping** (n.)

4.2.188   **peacemaker** (n.)

4.2.189   **peacemaking** (n.)

4.2.190   **peacetime** (n.)

4.2.191   **per annum** (adv.)

4.2.192   **per capita** (adv., adj.)

4.2.193   **Philippines**

4.2.194   **policy maker** (n.)

4.2.195   **policy making** (n.)

4.2.196   **policy-making** (adj.)

4.2.197   **post-**. Compound words with the prefix *post* are usually solid: postwar, postaxial, postmortem, *but* post-cold-war world or post–Cold War world. See also compound words (4.2.52).

4.2.198 **pre-**. Compound words with the prefix *pre* are usually solid: pre-existing, predetermined, prejudge, preempt. *But* pre-latency-period development. See also compound words (4.2.52).

4.2.199 **pro-**. Compound words with the prefix *pro* are usually solid: pro-government, pronuclear. See also compound words (4.2.52).

4.2.200 **proactive** (adj.)

4.2.201 **proactively** (adv.)

4.2.202 **problem solver** (n.)

4.2.203 **problem solving** (n.)

4.2.204 **problem-solving** (adj.)

4.2.205 **re-**. Compound words with the prefix *re* are usually solid: reedit, reeducate, reelect, reenlist, reequip, reexamine, reunify. See also compound words (4.2.52).

4.2.206 **real time** (n.)

4.2.207 **real-time** (adj.)

4.2.208 **real-world** (adj.)

4.2.209 **risk taking** (n.)

4.2.210 **risk-taking** (adj.)

4.2.211 **road map** (n.)

4.2.212 **sea-lane** (n.)

4.2.213 **sealift** (n., v.)

4.2.214 **sea power** (n.)

4.2.215 **self-**. Most *self-* compounds are hyphenated: self-reliant, self-sustaining, *but* selfless, selfsame. See also hyphenated compound words (3.2.8).

4.2.216 **semi-**. Compound words with the prefix *semi* are usually spelled solid: semifinal, semiofficial, *but* semi-indirect. See also compound words (4.2.52).

4.2.217 **semiannual**. See also semiannual (1.48).

4.2.218 **Shiite**

4.2.219 **short-range** (adj.)

4.2.220 **short term** (n.)

4.2.221 **short-term** (adj.)

4.2.222 **space-**. Compounds with this term are solid, open, and hyphenated: spaceman, spaceship, spaceflight, spacewalk (v.), space suit, space station, space walk (n.), space age, space power, space shuttle, space-age (adj.), space-time. See also compound words (4.2.52); hyphenated compound words (3.2.8).

4.2.223 **space lift** (n.)

4.2.224 **space-lift** (v., adj.)

4.2.225 **space power**

4.2.226 **standby** (n., adj., adv.)

4.2.227 **stand by** (v.)

4.2.228 **standoff** (n.)

4.2.229 **stand off** (v.)

4.2.230 **state of the art** (n.)

4.2.231 **state-of-the-art** (adj.)

4.2.232 **sub-**. Compound words with the prefix *sub* are usually written solid: subcommittee, subcontract, substandard, *but* sub-Saharan Africa. See also compound words (4.2.52).

4.2.233 **superpower** (n.)

4.2.234   **takeoff** (n.)

4.2.235   **take off** (v.)

4.2.236   **takeover** (n.)

4.2.237   **take over** (v.)

4.2.238   **test-fly** (v.)

4.2.239   **theater, theatre**. Shortened form of *theater of operations* or *theater of war*. Lowercase, as in European theater. Either spelling is standard; choose one, and use it consistently.

4.2.240   **third-**. Compound words with this term occur in all three stylings: third base, third baseman, third class (n.), third degree (n.), third grader, thirdhand (adj., adv.), third-class (adj.), third-degree (adj.). See also compound words (4.2.52); hyphenated compound words (3.2.8).

4.2.241   **trans-**. Words formed with the prefix *trans* are generally closed: transship, transcontinental, transoceanic. Compounds whose second element is a capitalized word are hyphenated: trans-America, *but* transatlantic. See also compound words (4.2.52); hyphenated compound words (3.2.8).

4.2.242   **tri-**. Compound words with the prefix *tri* are usually closed: tricolor, trilingual, tristate. See also compound words (4.2.52).

4.2.243   **U-boat**

4.2.244   **ultra-**. Most compounds with the prefix *ultra* are solid: ultramodern, ultrasonic, *but* ultra-atomic, ultra-German. See also compound words (4.2.52); hyphenated compound words (3.2.8).

4.2.245   **un-**. Most compounds with the prefix *un* are solid: unbiased, unsolved, unused. See also compound words (4.2.52).

4.2.246   **under-**. Most compounds with this term are solid: underbid, underdevelop, underestimate, underground, undersea, undersecretary, underreport. See also compound words (4.2.52).

4.2.247   **underway** (adj.)

4.2.248   **under way** (adv.)

4.2.249 **vice-**. Compounds with this term can be open, solid, or hyphenated: vice admiral, vice-chief, vice-commander, vice-marshal, vice-minister, vice president, vice squad, viceroyalty, vice-chairman, vice-consul. Hyphenate if the word is not in the dictionary. See also compound words (4.2.52); hyphenated compound words (3.2.8).

4.2.250 **vice versa** (adj.)

4.2.251 **Vietcong** (n., sing. and pl.)

4.2.252 **Vietminh** (n., sing. and pl.)

4.2.253 **walk-**. Most compounds with this term are either hyphenated or solid: walk-on (n.), walk-up (n.), walkout (n.), walkover (n.). See also compound words (4.2.52); hyphenated compound words (3.2.8).

4.2.254 **war-**. Compounds with this term occur in all three stylings: war chest, war power, war room, war zone, warlike, warpath, warplane, warship, wartime, war-game (v.). See also compound words (4.2.52); hyphenated compound words (3.2.8).

4.2.255 **war fighter** (n.)

4.2.256 **war fighting** (n.)

4.2.257 **war-fighting** (adj.)

4.2.258 **war-game** (v.) (e.g., to war-game an invasion)

4.2.259 **war game** (n.)

4.2.260 **war gamer** (n.)

4.2.261 **war gaming** (n.)

4.2.262 **war-gaming** (adj.)

4.2.263 **warhead** (n.)

4.2.264 **war making** (n.)

4.2.265 **war-making** (adj.)

4.2.266   **warplane** (n.)

4.2.267   **warship** (n.)

4.2.268   **wartime** (n.)

4.2.269   **wavelength(s)** (n.)

4.2.270   **well-**. Most compounds formed with *well* are either hyphenated or solid: well-being (n.), well-defined (adj.), well-grounded (adj.), well-intentioned (adj.), well-known (adj.), well-read (adj.), well-spoken (adj.), well-timed (adj.), wellborn (adj.), wellness (n.). Generally, you should hyphenate compounds with *well* before the noun: A well-known man came to my house. Do not use the hyphen when the expression carries a modifier: A very well known man made an unexpected appearance at the party. Do not use the hyphen when the compound follows the word it modifies: She is well known for her recipes. See also hyphenated compound words (3.2.8).

4.2.271   **weltanschauung** (n., often capitalized). Worldview.

4.2.272   **wide-**. Compounds beginning with this term occur in all three stylings: wide receiver (n.), wideawake (n.), widemouthed (adj.), widespread (adj.), wide-awake (adj.), wide-eyed (adj.), wide-spreading (adj.). See also compound words (4.2.52); hyphenated compound words (3.2.8).

4.2.273   **-wide**. Compounds ending in this term are written solid unless they are long and cumbersome (i.e., if the suffix follows most words of three or more syllables) or unless they include a proper noun: countrywide, nationwide, servicewide, statewide, theaterwide, worldwide, *but* university-wide, Chicago-wide, Air Force–wide. The hyphenated forms remain hyphenated both before and after the words they modify: The rule applied university-wide. See also compound words (4.2.52); hyphenated compound words (3.2.8).

4.2.274   **wingspan** (n.)

4.2.275   **wiretap** (n., v.)

4.2.276   **wiretapper** (n.)

4.2.277 **work-**. Compounds with this term occur in all three stylings: work ethic, workday, work-up (n.). See also compound words (4.2.52); hyphenated compound words (3.2.8).

4.2.278 **work-around** (n.)

4.2.279 **work around** (v.)

4.2.280 **workforce** (n.)

4.2.281 **work hour(s)** (n.). See also man-hour(s) (4.2.149).

4.2.282 **workload** (n.)

4.2.283 **worldview** (n.). See also weltanschauung (4.2.271).

4.2.284 **worldwide** (adj., adv.)

4.2.285 **year-**. Compounds beginning with this term occur in all three stylings: year of grace, yearbook, year-end. See also compound words (4.2.52); hyphenated compound words (3.2.8).

4.2.286 **zero** (n. sing.), **zeros** (n. pl.), also **zeroes** (n. pl.). See also 1.75.

4.2.287 **zero hour** (n.)

4.2.288 **zero-sum** (adj.)

4.3 *Numbers*

Spell out whole numbers zero through nine. Use figures for numbers greater than nine:

> Katie read three books in two months.
>
> The convention center can hold 5,000 people.

You may use figures followed by *million*, *billion*, and so forth to express large numbers:

> China has more than one (or 1) billion people.
>
> By the end of the year, the corporation was in debt by $2.3 million.

If a sentence contains several numbers, some of them 10 or above, follow the basic rule:

> We are authorized six officers, 39 enlisted personnel, and three civilians
> in our two squadrons.

The general rule for spelling numbers also applies to ordinal numbers. Either use *d* for both *second* and *third* or use *nd* and *rd* for *second* and *third*, respectively (placed on the line rather than written as superscripts). Choose one style, and use it consistently.

> Sergeant Adams conducted the 92d through 103d hours of the drill.
>
> The 122nd and 123rd days of the strike were marked by renewed violence.

Spell out any number that starts a sentence:

> Twelve people applied for the job.

Apply to adjective modifiers the rules for spelling out whole numbers zero through nine and for expressing large numbers:

four-mile hike	11-mile hike
five-day week	40-hour week
five-ton truck	9,000-ton ship
two (or 2)-million-member union	10-million-vote margin
four-year-old boy	zero-based budgeting

In mathematical, statistical, technical, or scientific texts, express physical quantities such as distances, lengths, areas, volumes, pressures, and so forth in figures:

60 miles	110 volts
15 yards	10 tons
40 acres	3 meters
3 1/3 cubic feet	45 pounds

In ordinary textual matter, apply the basic rule for the spelling of numbers:

Doris lost five pounds in a week.

John's car can barely go 60 miles an hour.

Spell out common fractions in textual matter:

More than one-third of the class failed the exam.

My brothers and I live within three and one-half miles of each other.

Use figures to express a combination of mixed numbers and whole numbers:

He typed the report on 8½-by-11-inch paper.

If you abbreviate a unit of measure, express the quantity with a figure:

9 mi.	35 mm
30 lb.	20 km

For two or more quantities, the abbreviation or symbol is repeated if it is closed up to the number, but not if it is separated:

35%–50%   2 x 5 cm

Use figures with symbols:

5½"   8° F

Use figures for decimal fractions:

He multiplied the number by 3.17.

In textual matter, use the word *percent* preceded by figures; in a table or chart, or in scientific or statistical text, you may use the symbol %.

1 percent

50 percent

Spell out or use figures for amounts of money in US currency in accordance with the basic rule. If you spell out the number, spell out the unit of currency; if you use figures, use the symbols $ or ¢:

> The commission raised the tax four cents.
> The club raised a total of $425.

Use a dollar sign, figures, and units of millions or billions to express large sums of money:

> Jim signed with the Atlanta Falcons for $3 million.

Use figures for fractional amounts over one dollar, like other decimal fractions. When you use whole-dollar amounts in the same context with fractional amounts, set the whole-dollar amounts with zeros after the decimal point:

> The music store sold CDs for $12.00 to $15.98.

In textual matter, indicate inclusive years as follows: *1900–1901*; *1907–8*; *1968–72* or *from 1968 to 1972* (never *from 1968–72*). In endnotes, use *1968–1972*. If you are composing a book title that includes dates, repeat all digits: *My High School Incarceration, 1965–1968*. However, do not alter a published title that includes abbreviated dates: *Clarkson's Antagonism, 1946–51*. In chapter titles, subheadings, and legends/captions, use the abbreviated form (in chapter 4, "From Meeting to Marriage, 1932–38").

Spell out references to particular centuries; spell out or use figures and apostrophes for references to decades:

> the twentieth century
> during the sixties and seventies
> the '60s and '70s

If you identify decades by their century, use figures:

> the 1880s and 1890s

Spell out times of day in even, half, and quarter hours:

> We went to the theater at a quarter after seven.
> The service starts at five o'clock.

Use figures to emphasize an exact time:

> The program is televised at 8:35 in the morning.

If you use the 24-hour system, do not punctuate between the hours and minutes:

The office opens at 0815.

Our duty hours are from 0730 to 1100 and from 1130 to 1600.

Use the following style for inclusive numbers:

First Number	Second Number	Examples
Less than 100	Use all digits	3–10, 71–72, 96–117
100 or multiple of 100	Use all digits	100–104, 600–613, 1100–1123
101 through 109 (in multiples of 100)	Use changed part only, omitting unneeded zeros	107–8, 505–17, 1002–6
110 through 199 (in multiples of 100)	Use two digits, or more if needed	321–25, 415–32, 1536–38, 1496–504, 14325–28, 11564–78, 13792–803

To avoid ambiguity, do not condense inclusive Roman numerals:

cvi–cix

Use an initial ordinal number (spelled out if ninth or less) to designate particular dynasties, governments, and governing bodies:

First Continental Congress	98th Congress
Third Reich	18th Dynasty
Sixth International	Fifth Republic

Use ordinal numbers to designate political divisions. The rule for spelling out numbers applies:

Fifth Congressional District
12th Precinct
Second Election District

Form the plurals of spelled-out numbers just as you would form the plurals of other nouns; add *s* (no apostrophe) to form the plurals of figures:

Hickock's hand contained two pairs: aces and eights.

The grades for the class were six 98s, three 100s, and the rest below 89.

In figures of one thousand or more (except page numbers), use a comma to set off groups of three digits, counting from the right:

2,000   34,000

In spelled-out fractional numbers, connect the numerator and the denominator with a hyphen unless either contains a hyphen:

three-fourths
six and seven-eighths
four and one-half years
seven and twenty-one thirty-seconds

4.3.1 **air force (numbered)**. See 4.3.19.

4.3.2 **caliber (of weapons)**. Use whole numbers or decimals, depending on the type of weapon: .38-caliber revolver, Colt .45, 9 mm automatic (no hyphen between a numeral and an abbreviation), 105 mm howitzer, 12-gauge shotgun.

4.3.3 **centuries and decades**. Spell out (in lowercase letters) references to particular centuries: eighth century, twentieth century. Use figures if decades are identified by their century: the 1880s and 1890s. See also numbers (4.3).

4.3.4 **chapter (numbers)**. Use Arabic figures for chapter numbers, even if the chapter numbers in the work cited are spelled out or in Roman numerals. The same principle holds true for other divisions of a book: part 1, section 3, book 7, volume 2.

4.3.5 **currency**. See money (4.3.18); numbers (4.3).

4.3.6 **dates**. Write exact dates in the sequence day-month-year, without commas. Spell out the month, use figures for the day, and use a four-digit year. When you use only the month and year, no commas are necessary.

FDR referred to 7 December 1941 as a day that would live in infamy.

The date March 2003 was special to her.

Do not use the all-numeral style for dates (3/11/50, etc.) in formal writing. However, in text discussing the events of [11 September 2001], the use of 9/11 is acceptable (Chicago, 6.115). If documentation, figures, and tables contain numerous dates, you may abbreviate certain months (Jan., Feb., Mar., Apr., May, June, July, Aug.,

Sept., Oct., Nov., Dec.) and use the sequence day-month-year without internal punctuation (7 Dec. 1941) to reduce clutter (Chicago, 9.39, 15.42, 17.225). Choose one style for the documentation, figures, and tables, and use it consistently. For inclusive numbers, see 4.3.

4.3.7   decades. Use figures if decades are identified by their century: the 1880s and 1890s. Spell out or use figures and apostrophes for particular decades: the eighties, the '80s. See also numbers (4.3).

4.3.8   dollars. See money (4.3.18); numbers (4.3).

4.3.9   Earth satellites. Use Arabic numerals in designations of artificial satellites: *Skylab 2*, *Voyager 2*. Earlier spacecraft used Roman numerals: *Gemini II*. Specific names of spacecraft and artificial satellites are italicized. See also spacecraft (4.4.21).

4.3.10   figures. See numbers (4.3) or illustrations (1.33), as appropriate.

4.3.11   fractions. See numbers (4.3).

4.3.12   highway (numbered). Use Arabic numerals to designate state, federal, and interstate highways: Interstate 85, Alabama 41.

4.3.13   hundreds. See numbers (4.3).

4.3.14   Mach 2 (etc.). Use numerals with "Mach."

4.3.15   measurements. Numerals precede abbreviations for units of measure:

3 mi.   50 lb.
55 mph   35 mm film

See also abbreviations (2.0); hyphenated compound words (3.2.8); numbers (4.3).

4.3.16   military time. Measured in hours numbered zero to 23 (e.g., 0100, 0800, 1600, 2300), from one midnight to the next; midnight is 0000, not 2400. No internal punctuation. See also numbers (4.3).

4.3.17   military units. *Air Force units*. Use Arabic numerals to designate units up to and including wings. Spell out the names of numbered air forces:

42d [or 42nd] Civil Engineer Squadron
31st Combat Support Group
22d [or 22nd] Fighter Wing
Twenty-third Air Force

Army units. Use Arabic numerals to designate units up to and including divisions. Write corps names with Roman numerals, and designate Army groups with Arabic numerals. Spell out the names of numbered armies:

2d [or 2nd] Armored Cavalry Regiment
210th Field Artillery Brigade
82d [or 82nd] Airborne Division
XVIII Airborne Corps
3d [or 3rd] Army Group
First Army

Navy units. Use Arabic numerals to designate the number of task forces; spell out fleet numbers:

Task Force 58
Fifth Fleet

Marine Corps units. Use the same designations as Army units.

For writing ordinal numbers (e.g., 2d or 2nd), see 4.3.

4.3.18   money. Use a dollar sign and numerals to express large sums of money. See also numbers (4.3).

Both companies agreed on a price of $2 million.

4.3.19   numbered air force. Spell out names of numbered air forces: Eighth Air Force, Twenty-third Air Force. Use figures for a smaller unit: 15th Air Group. See also military units (4.3.17).

4.3.20   percent. Always spell out *percent* in humanistic text, and precede it with Arabic numerals: a 3 percent increase. You may use the % symbol in tables and in scientific or statistical text. See also numbers (4.3).

4.3.21   quantities. See measurements (4.3.15); numbers (4.3).

4.3.22   satellites. See Earth satellites (4.3.9).

4.3.23   temperature. See numbers (4.3).

4.3.24   time. See military time (4.3.16); numbers (4.3).

4.3.25   units of measure. See measurements (4.3.15).

4.3.26 **weights and measurements**. See measurements (4.3.15); numbers (4.3).

4.3.27 **year**. Use figures to designate specific years unless the sentence begins with the year:

Nineteen forty-five was an eventful year.

World War II ended in 1945.

In informal contexts, you may abbreviate the full number of a particular year: the spirit of '76.

If you use the month with the year, do not use internal punctuation: The study began in May 1979. See also dates (4.3.6); numbers (4.3).

4.3.28 **zero, zeros (also zeroes)**. Use a 0 in tables to denote zero amount instead of using a dash or leaving the space blank.

4.4 *Italics*

Italicize titles and subtitles of published books, periodicals, pamphlets, manuals, proceedings and collections, newspapers, and sections of newspapers published separately, as well as abbreviations of those publications (*The Art of War, The United States Strategic Bombing Survey, USSBS, Fortune* 500, *Air and Space Power Journal, ASPJ*, etc.). If you are marking a manuscript by hand, use underlining to indicate italics.

Italicize titles of motion pictures, continuing television and radio series, long poems and musical compositions, plays, and computer/ video games. Put titles of TV shows, songs, and radio programs in Roman type and enclose them in quotation marks:

Casablanca	Handel's *Messiah*
public television's *Masterpiece Theater*	*N.Y.P.D. Blue*
public radio's *All Things Considered*	"In the Mood"
Paradise Lost	radio's "Christmas '99 at the
Tomb Raider: Chronicles	Kennedy Center"

If you use the names of newspapers, titles of books, or other italicized names in the plural, set the plural inflection in Roman type: There were five *Journal*s and two *Tribune*s on the shelf.

All punctuation marks should appear in the same font—Roman or italic—as the main or surrounding text, except for punctuation that belongs to a title or an exclamation in a different font (Chicago, 6.3).

> Smith played the title role in *Hamlet, Macbeth, and King Lear*; after his final performance, he announced his retirement.
>
> *A History of the United States Air Force, 1907–1957*
>
> Many editors admire *Wired Style*: it is both elegant and easy to use.
>
> *An Apache Life-way: The Economic, Social, and Religious Institutions of the Chiricahua Indians*
>
> What is meant by *random selection*?
>
> She is the author of *What's Next?*
>
> For light entertainment, he reads *King Lear*!
>
> The manual *Online!* is always at my elbow.
>
> We heard his cries of "*Help!*"

When a proper name is set in italics, the possessive ending (including the apostrophe) should be in Roman:

> the *Pueblo*'s captain

Parentheses and brackets should appear in the same font—Roman or italic—as the surrounding text, not in that of the material they enclose:

The Asian long-horned beetle (*Anoplophora glabripennis*) attacks maples.

The letter stated that my check had been "received [*sic*] with thanks."

When a phrase in parentheses or brackets appears on a line by itself, the parentheses or brackets are usually in the same font as the phrase (Chicago, 6.6):

[To be concluded]

Italicize the proper names of specific ships and submarines but not the accompanying abbreviations (e.g., USS, SS, HMS): HMS *Shannon*, SS *United States*, CSS *Alabama*, *Kiev*-class aircraft carrier. Capitalize but do not italicize the make of aircraft and ships and the names of space programs: Boeing 707, Project Apollo, ICBM, U-boat, DC-3.

Do not italicize titles of forms or put them in quotation marks. Instead, capitalize the main words: AF Form 673, Request to Issue Publication; AU Form 107, Request for Loan.

Italicize terms singled out as terms, and words referred to as words (see also quotation marks [3.2.14]):

The standard meaning of the term *leftist* is an adherent of the left wing of a party or movement.

Gladys cringed whenever anyone said *ain't*.

Italicize terms from languages other than English: *Leutnant, sic transit gloria mundi, aux armes*. However, if foreign terms have become familiar enough to be included in the main listing of a standard English dictionary, do not italicize them: weltschmerz, schadenfreude, ad hoc, fin de siècle, blitzkrieg, détente, déjà vu, perestroika, raison d'être, vis-à-vis.

Isolated foreign proper nouns are not italicized, even when cited as foreign terms:

Moscow (in Russian, Moskva) has been the capital of the Russian national state since the late fourteenth century.

When you provide a translation of the title of a foreign work in the text, use headline-style capitalization for the translated title but do not italicize it if the translation has not been published. However, use italics and headline style capitalization if the translation has been published. Enclose the translation in parentheses (Chicago, 10.6):

> Leonardo Fioravanti's *Compendio de i secreti rationali* (Compendium of Rational Secrets) became a best-seller.
>
> Proust's *À la recherche du temps perdu (Remembrance of Things Past)* was the subject of her dissertation.

When you cite the names of foreign institutions and businesses, capitalize them according to the usage of the country concerned. Unless they are transliterated from a non-Latin alphabet, do not italicize them. If you translate them, capitalize according to English usage (Chicago, 10.8).

> He is a member of the Société d'entraide des membres de l'ordre national de la Légion d'honneur.
>
> He was comforted to learn of the Mutual Aid Society for Members of the National Order of the Legion of Honor.

Italicize the names of legal cases when they are mentioned in text; in notes, they may be written in Roman; v. (versus) is preferably written in italics rather than Roman (Chicago, 8.88):

> *Brown v. Board of Education*

Italicize the shortened case name:

> *Miranda* or the *Miranda* case

You may occasionally use italics (not boldface) to emphasize a point:

> Effective *intelligence* is essential to military operations.

This device should be used sparingly. If your text is well written, the reader should have no problem determining what you consider important. See also emphasis (4.4.4).

4.4.1 **aircraft**. Do not italicize the class designation and class name of aircraft: F-15 Eagle, SR-71 Blackbird, Boeing 747. Italicize the name of a particular aircraft: *Spirit of St. Louis*, *Enola Gay*. See also italics (4.4).

4.4.2 **doctrine documents, instructions, manuals, pamphlets, and policy directives**. Italicize the title of the publication: Air Force Doctrine Document (AFDD) 2-4.3, *Education and Training*, AFDD 2-4.3 (subsequent reference); Air Force Instruction (AFI) 90-201, *Inspector*

General Activities, AFI 90-201; Air Force Manual (AFMAN) 10-100, *Airman's Manual*, AFMAN 10-100; Army Field Manual (FM) 27-10, *The Law of Land Warfare*, FM 27-10; Air Force Pamphlet (AFPAM) 36-2705, *Discrimination and Sexual Harassment*, AFPAM 36-2705; Air Force Policy Directive (AFPD) 36-4, *Air Force Civilian Training and Education*, AFPD 36-4.

4.4.3 **Earth satellites**. Specific names of spacecraft and artificial satellites are italicized: *Skylab 2, Voyager 2, Gemini II*.

4.4.4 **emphasis**. If you use italics to emphasize a word or words in a quotation, indicate that you have done so by adding a phrase such as "emphasis added" or "italics added" in parentheses following the quotation, as in this block quotation:

> Today we know that in wartime, *even in a conventional war of limited duration*, the two superpowers would fight a battle of attrition in space until one side or the other had wrested control. *And the winner would use the surviving space system to decide the contests on land and sea.*[7] (emphasis added)

Similarly, you may use an appropriate phrase to show that an italicized part of a quotation is not your doing but appears in the original, as in this run-in quotation:

> Gen Muir S. Fairchild noted that "each nation differs from all other nations, not only in its *degree* of vulnerability to air attack, but also in the *kind* of vulnerability" (emphasis in original).[21]

In a quotation with a mixture of original and added italics, use bracketed phrases immediately following the italicized passages to differentiate between them, as in this block quotation:

> Whether the means of protecting satellites will be adequate to *ensure the survivability* [emphasis added] of particular space-based BMD systems will depend in part on the kinds of systems deployed and in part on future Soviet antisatellite capabilities. *Insufficient information is now available to resolve the survivability question.*[24] [emphasis in original]

4.4.5 **epigraph**. Do not enclose an epigraph in quotation marks. Set it in italics in the same sized type as the text or in Roman a size smaller. See also 1.26.

4.4.6 **foreign terms**. See italics (4.4).

4.4.7 **forms (titles of)**. See italics (4.4).

4.4.8   **instructions**. See doctrine documents, instructions, manuals, pamphlets, and policy directives (4.4.2).

4.4.9   **journals**. Capitalize all main words of the title of a journal, and italicize both the full title and its abbreviation: *Air and Space Power Journal, ASPJ.*

4.4.10   **legal cases**. See italics (4.4).

4.4.11   **Luftwaffe**. No italics.

4.4.12   **magazines**. See italics (4.4); journals (4.4.9).

4.4.13   **manuals**. See doctrine documents, instructions, manuals, pamphlets, and policy directives (4.4.2).

4.4.14   **newspapers**. Italicize the names of newspapers: *Christian Science Monitor, Chicago Sun-Times.* In text, lowercase *the* and set it in Roman type: John read the *Wall Street Journal* religiously. Omit the definite article in note references to newspapers.

4.4.15   **pamphlets**. See doctrine documents, instructions, manuals, pamphlets, and policy directives (4.4.2).

4.4.16   **periodicals**. See italics (4.4); journals (4.4.9).

4.4.17   **policy directives**. See doctrine documents, instructions, manuals, pamphlets, and policy directives (4.4.2).

4.4.18   **see, see also**. Italicize these terms in an index but not in documentation (e.g., endnotes). Capitalize only when they begin a sentence.

4.4.19   **ships, names of**. See italics (4.4).

4.4.20   **sic (so; thus; in this manner)**. Use this term, italicized and bracketed, to indicate misspelling or improper usage in original text:

> The newscaster announced that "the pilot got out of his plane and laid [*sic*] down on the ground after his harrowing flight."

See also italics (4.4).

4.4.21   **spacecraft**. Italicize specific names of spacecraft and artificial satellites: *Gemini II, Apollo 11.* Also italicize names of particular space vehicles or components: *Eagle* (*Apollo 11* lunar module), *Columbia* (*Apollo 11* command module or space shuttle), and *Friendship 7* (Alan Shepard's Mercury capsule).

4.4.22   **Spetsnaz**. No italics.

4.4.23   **words as words**. Place words referred to as words in either italics or quotation marks: Tom wasn't sure whether *airpower* was one word or two.

4.5 *Display Dots*

Display dots are typographical devices used to emphasize specific items; they are not organizational devices used to subordinate textual elements. Use them when one item is no more important than the others or when the items do not show a sequence. Entries may be either complete or incomplete sentences but should be syntactically parallel and no longer than two or three sentences. Since display dots are used primarily for emphasis, use them sparingly and keep the information as short as possible. Indent each entry, and align run-over lines with the first word after the dot.

A special court-martial tries intermediate, noncapital offenses. It may be convened by any of the following:

- Any person who may convene a general court-martial.
- A commander empowered by the secretary of the Air Force unless otherwise directed.
- A commander of a wing, group, or separate squadron of the Air Force unless otherwise directed.

Specifically, the Office of Antiterrorism is charged with the following measures:

- Helping the newly formed Air Force Antiterrorism Council keep pace with related developments. Members of the council include senior officers of various deputy and assistant chiefs of staff, the Office of Security Police, the Office of the Judge Advocate General, and other agencies.
- Developing policy and guidance concerning security measures and precautions.
- Monitoring terrorist trends and providing information on such matters to interested agencies and commands.

The Camp David accords provide a process to facilitate the implementation of Resolution 242:

- a five-year transitional period for the West Bank and Gaza, providing full autonomy to the inhabitants;
- negotiations on the final status of the West Bank and Gaza and on a peace treaty between Jordan and Israel, to begin no later than three years into the transitional period;
- a framework for peace negotiations between Israel and Egypt; and
- principles for peace treaties between Israel and its other neighboring states.

The following engineering-data support centers have been established:

- The Cryptologic-Equipment Engineering-Data Support Center
- The Nuclear-Ordnance Engineering-Data Support Center

- The Air and Space Guidance and Metrological Engineering-Data Support Center
- Communications-Electronics Engineering-Data Support Center

In classified reports, material emphasized by display dots is considered part of the paragraph that introduced it, not as a separate paragraph.

5.0 Documentation

5.1 **notes**. Use the numbered-endnote system of documentation. Number the notes consecutively—beginning with 1—throughout a chapter and throughout the list of notes at the end of the chapter. Do not place note numbers after epigraphs, chapter or article titles, or subheadings. In text, put a superior (superscript) number at the end of a sentence or at least at the end of a clause, following any punctuation mark (except a dash) or a closing parenthesis. In the note itself, place the number (full-sized, not superscript) on the line and follow it with a period.

> Strategic considerations were often discussed, and Arnold urged abandonment of the "old 'island to island' theory."[6]
>
> Russia agreed to stop sales to Brazil—a longtime practice[7]—at the urging of the State Department.
>
> (When General Franks gave Bush a probable number of casualties, the president approved the attack.)[8]
>
> 3. Joseph S. Nye Jr., *The Paradox of American Power: Why the World's Only Superpower Can't Go It Alone* (New York: Oxford University Press, 2002), 8.

Include the following items in a full note reference to a book: (1) author's or editor's full name (as it appears on the title page), first name first, including military rank or academic title if included on title page, or name of institution responsible for writing the book (alternatively, the editor's name may follow the title of the book [see (3)]); (2) title of the book, including subtitle, in italics; (3) editor, compiler, or translator, if any; (4) edition, if not the first; (5) number of volumes (if referring to a multivolume work as a whole); (6) volume number of multivolume work (if referring to one specific volume); (7) title of volume, if applicable; (8) series, if any, and number in the series; (9) facts of publication—city where published, publisher, and date of publication, all in parentheses; (10) volume number (if citing a multivolume work, all of whose volumes have the same title), followed by a colon; (11) page number(s) of the specific citation; and (12) a URL for Internet sources or some indication of the medium cited (e.g., DVD, CD-ROM).

> 1. Walt Whitman, *Leaves of Grass* (Philadelphia: David McKay, 1891), 29, http://www.whitmanarchive.org/archive1/works/leaves/1891/text/frame set.html.

Include the following items in a full reference to an article in a periodical: (1) author's full name, first name first, including military rank or academic title if included in byline of article; (2) title of the article in quotation marks; (3) title of the periodical in italics; (4) volume number (no abbreviation for *volume*) and issue number (use *no.* for *number*) of the periodical; (5) date of the volume or of the issue (enclosed in parentheses and followed by a colon if volume and/or issue number are given; otherwise, the date is set off with a pair of commas); (6) page number(s) of the particular citation; and (7) a URL for online periodicals.

> 2. Col Rex R. Kiziah, "The Emerging Biocruise Threat," *Air and Space Power Journal* 17, no. 1 (Spring 2003): 85, http://www.airpower.maxwell.af.mil/ airchronicles/apj/apj03/spr03/spr03.pdf.

For subsequent references to a source, use only (1) the last name of the author; (2) *a shortened form of the title (if the full title is more than four words long), omitting an initial "A" or "The" (Chicago, 16.42);* (3) a comma; and (4) the page number of the reference. *If the notes include works by authors with the same last name, use the full name or initials in subsequent references to differentiate between them (Chicago, 16.44).*

> 3. Edward M. Coffman, *The War to End All Wars: The American Military Experience in World War I* (Madison, WI [or Wis. or Wisc.]: University of Wisconsin Press, 1986), 215.
> 4. Hunter Liggett, *Ten Years Ago in France* (New York: Dodd, Mead, 1928), 84.
> 5. Dr. Robin Higham and Dr. Mark P. Parillo, "Management Margin: Essential for Victory," *Aerospace Power Journal* 16, no. 1 (Spring 2002): 22, http://www.airpower.maxwell.af.mil/airchronicles/apj/apj02/spr02/spr02.pdf.
> 6. Maj David W. Coffman, *Operational Art and the Human Dimension of Warfare in the 21st Century* (Newport, RI [or R.I.]: Naval War College, 1911), 17.
> 7. Edward M. Coffman, *War to End All Wars*, 220.
> 8. Higham and Parillo, "Management Margin," 23.

The abbreviation *ibid.* (*ibidem*, "in the same place") refers to a single work cited in the note immediately preceding. Never use *ibid.* if more than one work is cited in the preceding note. Do not italicize this abbreviation in your notes. Do not use *op. cit.* (*opere citato*, "in the work cited") or *loc. cit.* (*loco citato*, "in the place cited"). Instead, use a shortened form of the citation. You may use *ibid.* within the note to indicate successive references to the same work.

> 7. Richard G. Davis, *Carl A. Spaatz and the Air War in Europe* (Washington, DC [or D.C.]: Office of Air Force History, 1993), 331.
> 8. Ibid., 301.
> 9. Gen Richard B. Myers, "A Word from the Chairman: Shift to a Global Perspective," *Air and Space Power Journal* 17, no. 3 (Fall 2003): 5, http://

www.airpower.maxwell.af.mil/airchronicles/apj/apj03/fal03/fal03. pdf. "By shifting our view from a regional to a global perspective, we will better comprehend and respond to America's security needs in the twenty-first century" (ibid., 8).

You may use *idem* ("the same") rather than repeating the author's name in subsequent references in one note to works by the same author. However, since the term is used so rarely, it might be better simply to repeat the author's last name.

> 10. Col Dennis M. Drew, "Inventing a Doctrine Process," *Airpower Journal* 9, no. 4 (Winter 1995): 43, http://www.airpower.maxwell.af.mil/ airchronicles/ apj/drew.pdf; and idem [or Drew], "Educating Air Force Officers," *Airpower Journal* 11, no. 2 (Summer 1997): 38, http://www .airpower.maxwell.af.mil/ airchronicles/apj/sum97/drew.pdf.

You may use a shortened form the first time a work is cited in a chapter's endnotes if a full citation for that work has appeared in the notes to a previous chapter. If the notes are far apart, you may use a cross-reference to help the reader locate the full reference (Chicago, 16.43).

> 11. Liggett, *Ten Years Ago in France*, 90 (see chap. 2, n. 2).

Always use Arabic figures for volume numbers even when they appear as Roman numerals in the book or journal itself.

Examples of full and shortened references:

> 3. Franz Schurman, *Imperial China: The Decline of the Last Dynasty and the Origins of Modern China* (New York: Vintage Books, 1967), 206–8.
>
> 4. John K. Fairbank, "The People's Middle Kingdom," *Foreign Affairs* 58 (1964): 943–68.
>
> 5. Capt Gerald G. O'Rourke, "Our Peaceful Navy," US Naval Institute *Proceedings*, April 1989, 79–83.
>
> 6. Franz Schurman, *Japan Today* (New York: Vintage Books, 1970), 97–100.
>
> 7. Schurman, *Imperial China*, 174. [Shortened form of note 3 with different page number.]
>
> 8. Ibid., 176. [All information the same as in the preceding note except page number.]
>
> 9. Carl von Clausewitz, *On War*, ed. and trans. Michael Howard and Peter Paret (Princeton, NJ [or N.J.]: Princeton University Press, 1976), 25.
>
> 10. James N. Stevens, *The Foundations of Communist China*, 2 vols. (Baltimore: Johns Hopkins University Press, 1969), 1:150.
>
> 11. Ibid., 2:96. [All information the same as in the preceding note except volume number and page number.]
>
> 12. Ibid., 147. [The same volume number as in the preceding note.]
>
> 13. Ibid. [The same page number as in the preceding note.]

In a work whose bibliography contains all of the material referred to in the notes, the notes may be presented in a concise format—even first citations—since the reader can refer to the bibliography for full details. In a work without a bibliography or whose bibliography does not contain all of the material referred to in the notes, first citations should contain full details (Chicago, 16.3). For the benefit of the reader, you may wish to include a brief explanatory statement preceding the first set of notes.

Bibliographic entry:

Reynolds, Col Richard T. *Heart of the Storm: The Genesis of the Air Campaign against Iraq.* Maxwell AFB, AL (or Ala.): Air University Press, 1995.

First note citation in a work with full bibliography:

Notes

(All notes appear in shortened form. For full details, see the appropriate entry in the bibliography.)

1. Reynolds, *Heart of the Storm,* 55.

First note citation in a work without full bibliography:

Notes

1. Col Richard T. Reynolds, *Heart of the Storm: The Genesis of the Air Campaign against Iraq* (Maxwell AFB, AL [or Ala.]: Air University Press, 1995), 55.

An interview with a person who prefers to remain anonymous or whose name the author does not wish to reveal may be cited in whatever form is appropriate in context. The absence of a name should be explained (e.g., "All interviews were conducted in confidentiality, and the names of interviewees are withheld by mutual agreement") (Chicago, 17.206).

10. Interview with health care worker, 10 August 1999.

See appendix A of this guide or the 15th edition of *The Chicago Manual of Style* for citations of public documents and unpublished materials.

5.2   **bibliography**. A bibliography is a list of books, articles, and other works used in preparing a manuscript. It immediately precedes the index and may be arranged alphabetically or divided into the kinds of materials used (books, theses and papers, government publications, periodicals, etc.). It may include only selected titles that may or may not be annotated.

An alphabetical list is the most common type of bibliography. Arrange all sources alphabetically by the last names of the authors, in a single list. When no author is given, use the first word of the title (other than an article, a coordinating conjunction, or a preposition) as the key word for alphabetizing. If a publication issued by an organization carries no author's name, use the name of the organization as the author, even if the organization is also the publisher.

In a lengthy bibliography, you may divide the references into kinds of sources (books, articles, newspapers, depositories, or collections). Whatever the arrangement, do not list any source more than once.

You may annotate the bibliography to direct the reader to other works or to briefly explain the contents, relevance, or value of specific sections of the book.

Invert the names of authors (i.e., last name first) and separate the various components of information with periods. The following are examples of citations in bibliographic format:

AFDD 1. *Air Force Basic Doctrine*, 17 November 2003.

AFPD 36-4. *Air Force Civilian Training, Education, and Development*, 12 February 2004.

Clausewitz, Carl von. *On War.* Edited and translated by Michael Howard and Peter Paret. Princeton, NJ (or N.J.): Princeton University Press, 1976.

Cressey, George B. *China's Geographic Foundations: A Survey of the Land and Its People.* New York: McGraw-Hill Book Co., 1934.

Cuskey, Walter R., Arnold William Klein, and William Krasner. *Drug-Trip Abroad: American Drug-Refugees in Amsterdam and London.* Philadelphia: University of Pennsylvania Press, 1972.

Drew, Col Dennis M. "Joint Operations: The World Looks Different from 10,000 Feet." *Airpower Journal* 2, no. 3 (Fall 1988): 4–16. http://www .airpower.maxwell.af.mil/airchronicles/apj/apj88/drew.html. [provide beginning and ending page numbers for journal articles]

Fairbank, John K. "The People's Middle Kingdom." *Foreign Affairs* 58 (June 1964): 943–68.

Hall, Col Brian K. "Air Expeditionary Access: The African Connection." *Air and Space Power Journal* 17, no. 3 (Fall 2003): 47–56. http:// www.airpower.maxwell.af.mil/airchronicles/apj/apj03/fal03/fal03.pdf (accessed 16 October 2003).

Schurman, Franz. *China Today.* New York: Vintage Books, 1970.

———. [use a three-em dash to indicate same author as in the immediately preceding entry] *Imperial China: The Decline of the Last Dynasty and the Origins of Modern China.* New York: Vintage Books, 1967.

Spencer, Scott. "Childhood's End." *Harper's*, May 1979, 16–19.

Stevenson, Adlai E., III. *The Citizen and His Government.* Austin, TX (or Tex.): University of Texas Press, 1984.

See appendix B and page 181 of this guide, as well as the 15th edition of *The Chicago Manual of Style* for more examples and specific rules for developing a bibliography.

5.3　**quotations**. Certain rules apply when you quote directly from the work of other writers. You should credit your source by identifying it in an endnote. If you quote at length from a copyrighted work, you should obtain written permission from the holder of the copyright (see also appendix C of this guide). *Although in a direct quotation the wording, spelling, capitalization, and internal punctuation of the original should be reproduced exactly, the following changes are generally permissible to make the passage fit into the syntax and typography of the surrounding text:*

1. *Single quotation marks may be changed to double, and double to single.*
2. *The initial letter may be changed to a capital or a lowercase letter.*
3. *The final period may be omitted or changed to a comma as required, and punctuation may be omitted where ellipsis points are used.*
4. *Original notes and note reference marks may be omitted unless omission would affect the meaning of the quotation. If an original note is included, the quotation should be set off as a block quotation, with the note in smaller type at the end, or the note may be summarized in the accompanying text. Authors may, on the other hand, add note references of their own within quotations.*
5. *Obvious typographic errors may be corrected silently (without comment or* sic) *unless the passage quoted is from an older work or a manuscript source where idiosyncrasies of spelling are generally preserved. If spelling and punctuation are modernized or altered for clarity, readers must be so informed in a note, in a preface, or elsewhere. (Chicago, 11.8)*

You may incorporate quotations in the text as a part of a sentence and enclose them in quotation marks or set them off from the text as a block quotation (see 5.4). If the quoted matter is eight or more lines or more than 100 words, you should usually set it off from the text.

Integrate short quotations into the text. When you use a quotation as part of a sentence, lowercase the initial letter and omit or change the end punctuation (if appropriate), even though the original is a complete sentence beginning with a capital letter. When the quotation is not dependent on the rest of the sentence, capitalize the initial letter (a comma rather than a colon is often used after *said, replied, asked,* and similar verbs). If a quotation that is only part of a sentence in the original forms a complete sentence as quoted, you may change a lowercase letter to a capital.

> Colonel Green emphasized that "the military plays an important role in the political arena."[7]

> Colonel Green said, "The military plays an important role in the political arena."[7]

> Colonel Green made the following statement: "Military [power] plays an important role in the political arena."[7]

5.4 **block quotations**. Use a block quotation for passages easily set apart from the text, eight or more typed lines, 100 words or more, or exceeding one paragraph. Indent from both sides and single-space. Do not use quotation marks to enclose the block quotation, and do not indent its paragraphs. Use double quotation marks to enclose a direct quotation within a block quotation. Skip a line between paragraphs. The block quotation should reflect the paragraphing of the original.

> In volume one of AFM 1-1, *Basic Aerospace Doctrine of the United States Air Force* (March 1992), Gen Merrill A. McPeak remarks,

>> The guidance this manual provides will be valuable to those in field units and to those in headquarters, to those in operations and to those in support areas, to those who understand air and space power and to those who are just learning. In short, this manual will be valuable to the entire force.

>> I expect every airman and, in particular, every noncommissioned and commissioned officer to read, study, and understand volume I and to become fully conversant with volume II. The contents of these two volumes are at the heart of the profession of arms for airmen.[1]

Unless you introduce a block quotation with thus, as follows, or other wording that requires a colon, you may precede the quotation with a period, although a colon is acceptable. Select either style, and use it consistently (Chicago, 11.22).

> This assumes that the costs of undertaking the first part of the conflict are "sunk" once the decision for armed intervention is made. One conflict scenario in particular illustrates this point.

>> Regime change is forced during the course of the initial conflict. Additional marginal losses occur in both the military and civilian populations. Postconflict losses are minimal but still happen due to incidents that arise during nation-building efforts. The costs of nation building are significant, but the total expense is likely to be less than that of the other scenarios.[22]

5.5   **credit line**. Identify the source of an illustration (see 1.33) with a credit line. Place it at the end of the caption/legend (see 1.18), in parentheses or in different type (or both), introduced by *reprinted from* or *adapted from*, depending upon whether you have copied the illustration or modified it, respectively:

> Figure 3. Competitive effects on general and administrative costs. (Adapted from Maj Paul G. Hough, "Financial Management for the New World Order," *Airpower Journal* 6, no. 3 [Fall 1992]: 51.)

A photographer's name occasionally appears in small type parallel to the bottom side of a photograph. For material that the author has obtained free and without restrictions, the word "courtesy" may appear in the credit line (*Chicago*, 12.42, 12.46):

> Photograph courtesy of Col Mike Schrieve
>
> Mayor Lunsford at the groundbreaking ceremony for the industrial plant, September 2002. Courtesy of Cathi Fredericks.

Photographs from Air Force or other government sources do not require a credit line although you may include one if you wish (e.g., USAF photo). If all photos derive from a single source, you may omit individual credit lines and simply include an appropriate statement on the disclaimer page (e.g., The photographs in this book are from US Air Force sources.).

Unless fair use applies [see appendix C], an illustration repro-duced from a published work under copyright requires permission (*Chicago*, 12.47):

> Reproduced by permission from T. R. Fehrenbach, *This Kind of War* (Washington, DC [or D.C.]: Brassey's, 2000), facing 237.

If you reproduce a table from another source, identify it below the body of the table, introduced by the word *Source(s)* (often in italics and followed by a colon). Since the word *source* lacks specificity, consider using *reprinted from* or *adapted from*, depending upon whether you have copied the table or modified it, respectively. Do not identify the source by placing a note number after either the table number or the table title and then including an endnote in the list of chapter notes. *A note applying to the table as a whole follows any source note, is unnumbered, and is introduced by the word Note and a colon (often in italics)* (*Chicago*, 13.46).

> *Reprinted from* Department of the Air Force, *Air Force Performance in Desert Storm* (Washington, DC [or D.C.]: Government Printing Office, April 1991); and author's collation of published data.
>
> *Note:* These figures represent the most reliable information currently available.

See also appendix C.

5.6 **plagiarism.** If you use someone else's writing as if it were your own, you have committed plagiarism. This serious offense not only can lead to a lawsuit but also can bring about severe professional repercussions for the plagiarist. If you use another person's wording or if you put another person's idea into your own words, you should identify the borrowed passage and credit the author in a note.

> Strategy [is] the art of distributing and applying military means to fulfill the ends of policy.
>
> —B. H. Liddell Hart, *Strategy*

If you use Liddell Hart's definition of strategy in your text with the intention of leading readers to believe that it is your own, you are guilty of plagiarism. Using another writer's exact wording is permissible only if you identify the passage in your text by enclosing it in quotation marks and including an endnote:

> Perhaps strategy is more properly defined as "the art of distributing and applying military means to fulfill the ends of policy."[2]

You should then credit your source by including a proper citation in your list of notes:

> 2. B. H. Liddell Hart, *Strategy*, rev. ed. (New York: Frederick Praeger, Inc., 1954), 335.

Similarly, you should identify and credit others' writing that you put in your own words (paraphrase). Paraphrasing, however, is not simply a matter of changing or rearranging a few words here and there; you must recast the passage:

> *unacceptable paraphrase:*
>
> Strategy is the art of applying and distributing military means to achieve the objectives of policy.[2]

acceptable paraphrase:

> B. H. Liddell Hart envisioned a country's military as an instrument for carrying out national policy. The purpose of strategy, then, is deciding how to use the military toward this end.[2]

Ideally, you should introduce your paraphrase so that the reader has no question about where your own commentary ends and where your paraphrase begins, as is the case in the example above (i.e., mentioning the author's name marks the beginning of the paraphrase, and the endnote number shows where it ends). See also quotations (5.3) and appendix C.

APPENDIX A

Note Citations

Examples of several categories of notes appear below. For other examples, see the 15th edition of *The Chicago Manual of Style*. Place notes at the end of each chapter—not at the bottom of the page or at the end of the book. For subsequent references, use *ibid.* or a shortened form of the note. Use *ibid.* to refer to the note immediately preceding (do not use *ibid.* if that note contains more than one citation). *You may use ibid. within the note to indicate successive references to the same work (Chicago, 16.48).*

> 7. Richard G. Davis, *Carl A. Spaatz and the Air War in Europe* (Washington, DC [or D.C.]: Office of Air Force History, 1993), 331.
> 8. Ibid., 301.
> 9. Gen Richard B. Myers, "A Word from the Chairman: Shift to a Global Perspective," *Air and Space Power Journal* 17, no. 3 (Fall 2003): 5, http://www.airpower.maxwell.af.mil/airchronicles/apj/apj03/fal03/fal03.pdf. "By shifting our view from a regional to a global perspective, we will better comprehend and respond to America's security needs in the twenty-first century" (ibid., 8).

For subsequent references to a source, use only the last name of the author followed by *a shortened form of the title (if the full title is more than four words long), omitting an initial "A" or "The" (Chicago, 16.42),* a comma, and the page number of the reference. *If the notes include works by authors with the same last name, use the full name or initials in subsequent references to differentiate between them (Chicago, 16.44).*

> 3. Edward M. Coffman, *The War to End All Wars: The American Military Experience in World War I* (Madison, WI [or Wis. or Wisc.]: University of Wisconsin Press, 1986), 215.
> 4. Hunter Liggett, *Ten Years Ago in France* (New York: Dodd, Mead, 1928), 84.
> 5. Dr. Robin Higham and Dr. Mark P. Parillo, "Management Margin: Essential for Victory," *Aerospace Power Journal* 16, no. 1 (Spring 2002): 22, http://www.airpower.maxwell.af.mil/airchronicles/apj/apj02/spr02/spr02.pdf.
> 6. Maj David W. Coffman, *Operational Art and the Human Dimension of Warfare in the 21st Century* (Newport, RI [or R.I.]: Naval War College, 1911), 17.
> 7. Edward M. Coffman, *War to End All Wars,* 220.
> 8. Higham and Parillo, "Management Margin," 23.

In a work whose bibliography contains all of the material referred to in the notes, the notes may be presented in a concise format—even first citations—since the reader can refer to the bibliography for full details. In a work without a bibliography or whose bibliography does not contain all of the material referred to in the notes, first citations should contain full details

(*Chicago*, 16.3). For the benefit of the reader, you may wish to include a brief explanatory statement preceding the first set of notes.

Bibliographic entry:

Reynolds, Col Richard T. *Heart of the Storm: The Genesis of the Air Campaign against Iraq*. Maxwell AFB, AL (or Ala.): Air University Press, 1995.

First note citation in a work with full bibliography:

Notes

(All notes appear in shortened form. For full details, see the appropriate entry in the bibliography.)

1. Reynolds, *Heart of the Storm*, 55.

First note citation in a work without full bibliography:

Notes

1. Col Richard T. Reynolds, *Heart of the Storm: The Genesis of the Air Campaign against Iraq* (Maxwell AFB, AL [or Ala.]: Air University Press, 1995), 55.

You may use a shortened form the first time a work is cited in a chapter's endnotes if a full citation for that work has appeared in the notes to a previous chapter. If the notes are far apart, you may use a cross-reference to help the reader locate the full reference (*Chicago*, 16.43).

11. Liggett, *Ten Years Ago in France*, 90 (see chap. 2, n. 2).

Books

One author

1. Gen William C. Westmoreland, *A Soldier Reports* (Garden City, NY [or N.Y.]: Doubleday & Co., 1976), 112, 195–96. [Reproduce the author's name as it appears on the title page.]

Two authors

2. John W. Masland and Laurence I. Radway, *Soldiers and Scholars: Military Education and National Policy* (Princeton, NJ [or N.J.]: Princeton University Press, 1957), 117–21. [List the authors' names in the order in which they appear on the title page.]

Three authors

3. Robert Strausz-Hupe, William R. Kintner, and Stefan T. Possony, *A Forward Strategy for America* (New York: Harper & Bros., 1961), 117. [List the authors' names in the order in which they appear on the title page.]

More than three authors

4. Gerald Pomper et al., *The Election of 1976* (New York: McKay, 1977), 61. [Give the name of the author listed first on the title page followed by "et al." or "and others."]

5. Pomper et al., *Election of 1976*, 60. [shortened form]

No author given

6. *Soviet Military Power* (Washington, DC [or D.C.]: Government Printing Office, 1983), 13–18. [Do not use *Anonymous* or *Anon.*]

Editor, compiler, or translator

7. Alfred Goldberg, ed., *A History of the United States Air Force, 1907–1957* (Princeton, NJ [or N.J.]: D. Van Nostrand, 1957), 7. [Use the name of the editor, compiler, or translator in place of the author when no author's name appears on the title page.]

8. Goldberg, *History of the United States Air Force*, 10. [shortened form; omit the abbreviation for editor]

9. J. P. Mayer, *Alexis de Tocqueville: Democracy in America*, trans. George Lawrence (New York: Doubleday & Co., 1969), 648. [When the author's name appears on the title page, place the name of the editor, compiler, or translator after the title, preceded by *ed. [edited by]*, *comp. [compiled by]*, or *trans. [translated by]*.]

10. Carl von Clausewitz, *On War*, ed. and trans. Michael Howard and Peter Paret (Princeton, NJ [or N.J.]: Princeton University Press, 1976), 145–47.

11. Marshal Foch, *The Principles of War*, trans. Hilaire Belloc (London: Chapman & Hall, Ltd., 1918), 7, 18–19.

Multivolume works and series

12. Wesley Frank Craven and James Lea Cate, eds., *The Army Air Forces in World War II*, vol. 2, *Europe: Torch to Pointblank, August 1942 to December 1943* (1949; new imprint, Washington, DC [or D.C.]: Office of Air Force History, 1983), 288–95. [One volume in the series.]

13. Wesley Frank Craven and James Lea Cate, eds., *The Army Air Forces in World War II*, 7 vols. (1948–1958; new imprint, Washington, DC [or D.C.]: Office of Air Force History, 1983). [Entire series.]

14. Winston S. Churchill, *The Second World War*, vol. 4, *The Hinge of Fate* (Boston: Houghton Mifflin, 1948), 521.

15. Warren A. Trest, *Military Unity and National Policy: Some Past Effects and Future Implications*, CADRE Paper Special Series: The Future of the Air Force, no. AU-ARI-CPSS-91-7 (Maxwell AFB, AL [or Ala.]: Air University Press, December 1991), 12.

Association or institution as author

16. Gates Commission, *The Report of the President's Commission on an All-Volunteer Armed Force* (Washington, DC [or D.C.]: Government Printing Office, 1970), 3–9.

17. Department of Health, Education, and Welfare, *Work in America* (Cambridge, MA [or Mass.]: MIT Press, 1973), 104–6.

Work of one author in a work edited by another

18. Col John A. Warden III, "Air Theory for the Twenty-first Century," in *Challenge and Response: Anticipating US Military Security Concerns*, ed. Dr. Karl P. Magyar et al. (Maxwell AFB, AL [or Ala.]: Air University Press, August 1994), 320–21. [If you are citing the entire chapter or contribution, include inclusive page numbers.]

19. Warden, "Air Theory," 325. [shortened form]

20. Dr. Lewis B. Ware, "Regional Study 1: Conflict and Confrontation in the Post-Cold-War Middle East," in *Challenge and Response*, 49. [When you cite a different chapter/contribution in the same book as previously cited, include a shortened citation for that book.]

21. Capt John T. Folmar, "Desert Storm Chapstick," in *From the Line in the Sand: Accounts of USAF Company Grade Officers in Support of Desert Shield/Desert Storm*, ed. Capt Michael P. Vriesenga (Maxwell AFB, AL [or Ala.]: Air University Press, March 1994), 19–20.

Edition

22. John N. Hazard, *The Soviet System of Government*, 5th ed. (Chicago: University of Chicago Press, 1980), 23–25.

23. Norbert Weiner, *The Human Use of Human Beings: Cybernetics and Society*, 2d [or 2nd] ed. rev. (Garden City, NY [or N.Y.]: Doubleday, 1951), 68–71.

24. Weiner, *Human Use of Human Beings*, 74. [shortened form]

Reprint editions

25. Neil Harris, *The Artist in American Society: The Formative Years, 1790–1860* (1966; repr., Chicago: University of Chicago Press, 1982), 43–44.

26. Giulio Douhet, *The Command of the Air*, trans. Dino Ferrari (1942; new imprint, Washington, DC [or D.C.]: Office of Air Force History, 1983), 67.

Periodicals

Volume number not shown

27. "Congress Sends Nixon a Message," *Newsweek*, 19 November 1973, 39.

28. TSgt Jim Katzaman, "Basics of Bombing," *Airman*, June 1986, 8–12.

29. "Unions Are Alien to Our Defense System," *The Retired Officer*, May 1976, 25.

30. "Currents in the News," *U.S. News and World Report*, 11 February 1980, 5.

31. Jay Finegan, "Struggling with Inflation," *Times Magazine* (supplement to *Air Force Times*), 1 September 1980, 4.

Volume number shown

32. Col Richard F. Rosser, "American Civil-Military Relations in the 1980s," *Naval War College Review* 24, no. 10 (June 1972): 14–15.

33. Donald S. Zagoria, "China's Quiet Revolution," *Foreign Affairs* 62, no. 4 (Spring 1984): 879–904.

34. Philip Handler, "The American University Today," *American Scientist* 64, no. 3 (May–June 1976): 254–57.

35. Franklin D. Margiotta, "A Military Elite in Transition: Air Force Leaders in the 1980s," *Armed Forces and Society* 2, no. 2 (Winter 1976): 155–84.

36. Margiotta, "Military Elite in Transition," 176. [shortened form]

Newspaper Items

Editorial

37. Editorial, *Atlanta Constitution*, 19 June 1986. [Omit the initial *the* from titles of English language newspapers.]

News story

38. S. Fred Singer, "What Is Happening to World Oil?" *Wall Street Journal*, 10 March 1982.

39. William Robbins, "Big Wheels: The Rotary Club at 75," *New York Times*, Sunday, 17 February 1980, sec. 3.

40. Lt Gen Murphy A. Cheaney, "Military's Quality Medical Care for a Healthy Army," *Washington Times*, 16 December 1985, final edition.

Encyclopedia/Dictionary Articles

41. *Encyclopaedia Britannica*, 15th ed., s.v. "canning, commercial." [Cite the item, preceded by *s.v.* (*sub verbo*, "under the word").]

42. *Dictionary of American Biography*, s.v. "Wadsworth, Jeremiah."

Historical Studies

43. Robert T. Finney, *History of the Air Corps Tactical School, 1920–1940*, USAF Historical Study 100 (Maxwell AFB, AL [or Ala.]: USAF Historical Division, Air University, 1955), 35–38.

44. R. Earl McClendon, *Autonomy of the Air Arm* (Maxwell AFB, AL [or Ala.]: Documentary Research Division, Air University, 1954), 16–21.

45. Chase C. Mooney and Martha E. Layman, *Organization of Military Aeronautics, 1907–1935*, Army Air Forces Historical Study 25 (Washington, DC [or D.C.]: Army Air Forces Historical Division, 1944), 29–32.

46. Herman S. Wolk, *USAF Plans and Policies: Logistics and Base Construction in Southeast Asia, 1967* (Washington, DC [or D.C.]: Office of Air Force History, 1968), 36–39.

47. Thomas H. Greer, *The Development of Air Doctrine in the Army Air Arm, 1917–1941*, USAF Historical Study 89 (Maxwell AFB, AL [or Ala.]: USAF Historical Division, Air University, 1955), 9–10.

Staff Studies

48. Evaluation Division, Air University, Analyzing the USAF Publications System for Producing Manuals, staff study, 13 July 1948.

49. Col Herbert V. Staudenmaier, CONUS Aeromedical Evacuation Study, staff study, 31 March 1983.

50. Col Charles G. Williamson, chief, Status of Operations Division, Directorate of Bombardment, Headquarters Army Air Forces, to Directorate of Bombardment, Headquarters Army Air Forces, Status of Operations Report, staff study, 3 March 1943.

51. Williamson, Status of Operations Report. [shortened form]

Unit and Staff Office Histories

52. History, Deputy Chief of Staff for Plans and Programs, Directorate of Plans, Headquarters USAF, July–December 1958, 114, 163–64.

53. History, Research Studies Institute, July–December 1959, 1.

54. History of the Office of the Inspector General USAF, Directorate of Special Investigations, 1 January–30 June 1963, 45–47.

55. History, Tactical Air Command, 1 July–31 December 1953, 193–94.

Reports

Published

56. Department of Commerce, *Management of Internet Names and Addresses*, US Government White Paper (Washington, DC [or D.C.]: Department of Commerce, June 1998), 2.

57. United States Department of State, *The China White Paper, August 1949* (Stanford CA [or Calif.]: Stanford University Press, [1967]), 7.

58. John Erickson, *The Soviet Military, Soviet Policy, and Soviet Politics*, USSI Report 73-3 (Washington, DC [or D.C.]: United States Strategic Institute, 1973), 5.

59. Richard V. L. Cooper, *Military Manpower and the All-Volunteer Force*, RAND Report R-1450-ARPA (Santa Monica, CA [or Calif.]: RAND, September 1977), 86–94.

60. Comptroller General of the United States, *Report to the Congress: Student Attrition at the Five Federal Service Academies* (Washington, DC [or D.C.]: General Accounting Office, 1976), 16–23.

61. Nancy Guinn, *Identification of Service Irritants*, AFHRL-TR-75-52 (Brooks AFB, TX [or Tex.]: Air Force Systems Command, 1973).

62. James E. Dougherty and Diane K. Pfaltzgraff, *Eurocommunism and the Atlantic Alliance*, special report (Cambridge, MA [or Mass.]: Institute for Foreign Policy Analysis, 1977), 6.

63. Department of Defense, *Annual Report of the Secretary of Defense and the Annual Reports of the Secretary of the Army, Secretary of the Navy, and Secretary of the Air Force, July 1, 1958 to June 30, 1959* (Washington, DC [or D.C.]: Government Printing Office, 1960), 44.

64. Maj Mark A. Cochran, *Unit-Level Automation for Air Force Contingency Operations in Low-Intensity Conflict*, Research Report no. AU-ARI-91-4 (Maxwell AFB, AL [or Ala.]: Air University Press, June 1992), 21.

Unpublished

65. Maj John B. Hungerford Jr., "Organization for Military Space: A Historical Perspective," Research Report no. 82-1235 (Maxwell AFB, AL [or Ala.]: Air Command and Staff College, 1982), 9–19.

66. Report of Air Corps Board, "Revision of Field Service Regulations," study no. 45, 15 November 1983, 2.

67. Report of the General Headquarters Air Force (Provisional) 1933, ca. 20 July 1933.

Unpublished Papers

68. Richard K. Betts, "Soldiers, Statesmen, and Resort to Force: American Military Influence in Crisis Decisions, 1945–1976" (PhD diss., Harvard University, 1975), 78–86.

69. Betts, "Soldiers, Statesmen, and Resort to Force," 80. [shortened form]

70. Dorothy Ross, "The Irish-Catholic Immigrant, 1880–1900: A Study in Social Mobility" (master's thesis, Columbia University, n.d.), 142–55.

71. P. Thomas, "Utilization of Enlisted Women in the Military" (paper presented at the RAND Conference on Defense Manpower, Santa Monica, CA [or Calif.], February 1976), 8.

72. Thomas, "Utilization of Enlisted Women," 7. [shortened form]

73. Deborah D. Lucki and Richard W. Pollay, "Content Analyses of Advertising: A Review of the Literature" (working paper, History of Advertising Archives, Faculty of Commerce, University of British Columbia, Vancouver, 1980).

Manuscript Collections

Full identification of most unpublished material usually requires giving the title and date of the item, series title (if applicable), name of the collection, and name of the depository. Except for placing the cited item first (in a note), there is no general agreement on the sequence of the remaining elements in the citation. Whatever sequence is adopted, however, should be used consistently (Chicago, 17.222).

74. James Oglethorpe to the Trustees, letter, 13 January 1733, Phillipps Collection of Egmont Manuscripts, 14200:13, University of Georgia Library. (*Chicago*, 17.223)

75. Alvin Johnson, memorandum, 1937, file 36, Horace Kallen Papers, YIVO Institute, New York. (*Chicago*, 17.223)

76. George Creel to Colonel House, letter, 25 September 1918, Edward M. House Papers, Yale University Library. (*Chicago*, 17.230)

77. Undated correspondence between French Strother and Edward Lowry, container 1-G/961 600, Herbert Hoover Presidential Library, West Branch, IA [or Iowa]. (*Chicago*, 17.230)

78. Joseph Purcell, "A Map of the Southern Indian District of North America" [ca. 1772], MS 228, Ayer Collection, Newberry Library, Chicago. (*Chicago*, 17.230)

79. Joseph Dinkel, description of Louis Agassiz written at the request of Elizabeth Cary Agassiz, Agassiz Papers, Houghton Library, Harvard University. (*Chicago*, 17.231)

Legal Citations

The examples of legal citations included here assume inclusion in a non-legal work and, therefore, have been adapted to the style of documentation presented in this appendix. Thus, the format for citations of legal books/treatises and articles in periodicals is the same as that shown in the appropriate sections of this appendix. For citations styled for inclusion in legal works, see the 15th edition of *The Chicago Manual of Style*, 17.275.

80. *AT&T Corporation v. Iowa Utilities*, in *United States Supreme Court Reports*, vol. 525 (1999), 366.

81. *Old Chief v. United States*, in *Supreme Court Reporter*, vol. 117 (1997), 644.

82. *United States v. Dennis*, in *Federal Reporter*, vol. 183 (2d [or 2nd] US Circuit Court of Appeals, 1950), 201.

83. *Brown v. Board of Education*, in *Federal Supplement*, vol. 98 (US District Court, Kansas, 1951), 797.

84. *Lugosi* [plaintiff] *v. Universal* [defendant], in *California Reports*, 3d [or 3rd] series, vol. 25 (California Supreme Court, 1976), 813 [page].

85. *Daniels v. Weigum*, in *California Appellate Reports*, 2d [or 2nd] series, vol. 194 (California Court of Appeals, 1961), 620.

86. *United States v. Dennis*, 202. [shortened form]

Public Documents

When you use an endnote citing congressional hearings and other public documents, include the following information:

1. Author (name of house, committee, and subcommittee if any)
2. Title of document
3. Number of Congress and session number
4. Date of publication (year)
5. Part and number of report or document, if applicable
6. Page number(s)

Sometimes you may need to include additional information. Take all information from the title page of the document.

Bills, reports, and miscellaneous documents

87. House, *A Bill to Require Passenger-Carrying Motor Vehicles Purchased for Use by the Federal Government to Meet Certain Safety Standards*, 86th Cong., 1st sess., 1959, HR 1341, 1–4.

88. House, *Organization and Management of Missile Programs, Eleventh Report by the Committee on Government Operations*, 86th Cong., 1st sess., 1959, HR 1121, 154–56.

89. House, *Organization and Management*, 155. [shortened form]

90. House Committee on Education and Labor, *White House Conference on Aging: Report to Accompany S. J. Res. 117*, 90th Cong., 2d [or 2nd] sess., 1 May 1968, 5.

91. Senate, *Report of the Federal Trade Commission on Utility Corporations*, 70th Cong., 1st sess., 1935, S. Doc. 92, pt. 71A.

92. House, *United States Defense Policies in 1958*, 86th Cong., 1st sess., 1959, H. Doc. 227, 114.

93. HR Rep. 871, 78th Cong., 1st sess., 1943, 49.

94. Senate, *Documents on the International Aspects of the Exploration and Use of Outer Space, 1954–1962*, 88th Cong., 1st sess., 1963, S. Doc. 18, 55–56.

95. Senate Committee on Foreign Relations, *United States Foreign Policy*, 86th Cong., 2d [or 2nd] sess., 1960, Committee Print, 1:729.

96. House Committee on Foreign Affairs, *Central America, 1981: Report to the Committee on Foreign Affairs*, prepared by Hon. Gerry E. Studds, 97th Cong., 1st sess., 1981, Committee Print, 31.

97. House Committee, *Central America, 1981*, 30. [shortened form]

98. Department of State, *American Foreign Policy, Current Documents, 1958* (Washington, DC [or D.C.]: Government Printing Office, 1962), 1413.

Hearings

99. Senate, *Study of Air Power: Hearings before the Subcommittee on the Air Force of the Committee on Armed Services*, 84th Cong., 2d [or 2nd] sess., 1956, 52.

100. Senate, *Study of Air Power*, 1727. [shortened form]

101. Senate, *Investigation of Governmental Organization for Space Activities: Hearings before the Subcommittee on Governmental Activities of the Committee on Aeronautical and Space Science*, 86th Cong., 1st sess., 1959, 379–80.

102. House, *Department of Defense Appropriations for 1954: Hearings before the Subcommittee of the Committee on Appropriations*, 83d [or 83rd] Cong., 1st sess., 1953, 317.

103. House, *DOD Appropriations for 1954*, 289–91. [shortened form]

104. House, *Inquiry into Operations of the United States Air Services: Hearings before the Select Committee on Inquiry into Operations of the United States Air Services*, 69th Cong., 2d [or 2nd] sess., 1925, pt. 4:2269–70.

Congressional bills and resolutions

Known as public laws or statutes, bills and resolutions first appear in the *Congressional Record*, then in *United States Statutes at Large*, often in the *United States Code Annotated*, and finally in the *United States Code.*

105. *Food Security Act of 1985*, HR 2100, 99th Cong., 1st sess., *Congressional Record* 131 (8 October 1985): H8461.

106. HR 11818, 89th Cong., 1st sess., 1956, sec. 301(a).

107. S. Res. 218, 83d [or 83rd] Cong., 2d [or 2nd] sess., 1954.

108. *Atomic Energy Act of 1946*, Public Law 585, 79th Cong., 2d [or 2nd] sess. (1 August 1946), 12, 19.

109. *Atomic Energy Act of 1946, US Statutes at Large* 60 (1947): 767, 774. [Citations to the statutes are to volume, year, and page number.]

110. *Declaratory Judgment Act, US Code*, vol. 28, secs. 2201–2 (1952). [Citations to the code are always to section number, not page.]

111. *Declaratory Judgment Act*, secs. 2201–2. [shortened form]

Executive department documents

112. Department of Defense, *Profile of American Youth: 1980 Administration of the Armed Services Vocational Aptitude Battery* (Washington, DC [or D.C.]: Office of the Assistant Secretary of Defense [Manpower, Reserve Affairs and Logistics], March 1982), 19.

113. Department of Defense, *Profile of American Youth*, 23. [shortened form]

114. Department of Defense, *Official Guard and Reserve Manpower Strengths and Statistics, Fiscal Year 1985 Summary* (Washington, DC [or D.C.]: Assistant Secretary of Defense [Reserve Affairs], n.d.), 8.

115. Department of Defense, *Official Guard and Reserve*, 16. [shortened form]

Presidential proclamations, executive orders, other documents

116. President, Proclamation, "Supplemental Quota on Imports of Long-Staple Cotton," *Federal Register* 15, no. 196 (10 October 1950): 127, microfiche.

117. Executive Order 9877, Functions of the Armed Services, 26 July 1947.

118. EO 9877, Functions of the Armed Services. [shortened form]

119. *Public Papers of the Presidents of the United States: Dwight D. Eisenhower, 1957* (Washington, DC [or D.C.]: Government Printing Office, 1958), 796.

120. *Public Papers: Eisenhower*, 274–90. [shortened form]

121. Statement of the president, 26 January 1968, in *Weekly Compilation of Presidential Documents* 4, no. 4 (29 January 1968): 133.

122. UN General Assembly Resolution 1721 (XVI), "International Cooperation in the Peaceful Uses of Outer Space," 20 December 1961.

Classified Sources

Mark classified documents with the classification of the title (immediately following the title) and with the overall classification of the document (at the end of the publication data). If you take unclassified information from a classified source, put a statement to that effect after the overall classification marking.

123. TAF SON 302-81, *Statement of Operational Need for Night Attack Capabilities* (U), 2 November 1982. (Secret)

124. Assistant Chief of Staff, Intelligence, "Linebacker II: 18–29 December 72" (U), supporting document III-K1. (Top Secret) Information extracted is unclassified.

125. Robert L. Faloon, *Strategic Air Defense in Nuclear War* (U) (Maxwell AFB, AL [or Ala.]: Air University Press, 1983), 37. (Secret) Information extracted is unclassified.

Declassified Sources

126. Central Intelligence Agency, *National Intelligence Estimate Number 11-5-57* (Washington, DC [or D.C.]: Central Intelligence Agency, 1957), 62. Document is now declassified.

Letters, E-Mails, and Indorsements

127. Maj W. G. Kilner, executive, Office of Chief of Air Service, to commandant, Air Service Tactical School, letter, 12 April 1925.

127a. Kilner to commandant, letter. [shortened form]

128. Lt Col C. C. Culver to chief of Air Corps, letter, 9 June 1928; 1st ind., Maj L. W. McIntosh, executive, Office of the Chief of Air Corps, to commandant, Air Corps Tactical School, 1 September 1928.

129. The Adjutant General to commanding generals, all corps areas et al., letter, 31 December 1934.

130. Capt Harry A. Johnson, Command and General Staff School, to chief, Air Corps, letter, 18 January 1935; 2d [or 2nd] ind., Lt Col H. A. Pratt, chief, Air Corps, Materiel Division, to chief, Air Corps, 16 February 1935; 3d [or 3rd] ind., Col A. G. Fisher, president, Air Corps Board, to chief, Air Corps, 15 July 1945.

130a. Maj John Smith, chief, Office of Public Affairs, Maxwell AFB, AL, to the author, e-mail, 20 November 2005.

130b. Smith to the author, e-mail. [shortened form]

Memorandums

Regular memorandum

131. Lt Col G. W. Bundy, War Plans Division, War Department General Staff, to Lt Col Clayton J. Bissell, War Plans Division, memorandum, 18 July 1941.

132. Col William W. Momyer, deputy commandant for evaluation, Air War College, to Maj Gen John DeF. Barker, deputy commanding general, Air University, memorandum, 17 September 1952.

133. Momyer to Barker, memorandum. [shortened form]

Draft memorandum

134. Chief, Air Corps, to chief of staff, Army, draft memorandum, 28 March 1938.

Memorandum of understanding

135. Secretary of the Army to secretary of the Air Force, memorandum of understanding, 2 October 1951.

Memorandum for record

136. Gen Nathan F. Twining, vice-chief of staff, US Air Force, memorandum for record, 17 November 1950.

Messages

137. Message, TST-587, Joint Chiefs of Staff, to commanding general, Strategic Air Command, 13 April 1949.

138. Message, AFCVC-51413, US Air Force to commanding general, Far East Air Forces, 14 August 1950.

139. Message, 281415Z OCT 90, US Air Force to commanding general, Far East Air Forces, 28 October 1990.

Manuals, Instructions, Directives, and Other Publications

140. Air Force Doctrine Document (AFDD) 1, *Air Force Basic Doctrine*, 17 November 2003, 3.

141. AFDD 1, *Air Force Basic Doctrine*, 5. [shortened form]

142. War Department, *Field Service Regulations, United States Army* (Washington, DC [or D.C.]: Government Printing Office, 1924), 11, 21–24.

143. War Department Training Regulation (WDTR) 440-15, *Employment of the Air Forces of the Army*, 15 October 1935.

144. WDTR 440-15, *Employment of the Air Forces*. [shortened form]

145. Air Force Instruction (AFI) 90-901, *Operational Risk Management*, 1 April 2000.

146. Air Force Pamphlet (AFPAM) 36-106, *Supervisor's Records*, 20 December 1993.

147. AFDD 2-5.3, *Psychological Operations*, 27 August 1999.

148. DOD Directive (DODD) 5015.2, *DOD Records Management Program*, 6 March 2000.

149. Air Force Manual (AFMAN) 36-505, *Skill Coding*, 1 August 1996.

150. Maj Gary Ambrose, Staff Summary Sheet, Memorandum of Agreement on USAF Air Refueling Support for Navy Operations, 13 December 1985.

151. *Air Force Policy Letter for Commanders: Supplement*, February 1970, 2–6.

Source Cited/Quoted in Another Source

152. Quoted in George E. Lowe, *The Age of Deterrence* (Boston: Little, Brown & Co., 1964), 232.

153. Quoted in Lowe, *Age of Deterrence*, 234. [shortened form]

154. Quoted in Samuel P. Huntington, "Democracy Fights a Limited War: Korea, 1950–1953," in *Major Crises in American History: Documentary Problems*, ed. Merrill F. Peterson and Leonard W. Levy (New York: Harcourt, Brace and World, 1962), 2:481.

155. Letter of Secretary of Defense Robert McNamara to Cong. Robert Miller, 3 November 1961, in House, *Sundry Legislation Affecting the Naval and Military Establishment, 1963: Hearings before the Committee on Armed Services*, 88th Cong., 1st sess., 1963, 2729–30.

156. Statement of Lt Gen Paul Gorman, director for plans and policy, Organization of the Joint Chiefs of Staff, in Senate, *Department of Defense Authorization for Appropriations for Fiscal Year 1982: Hearings before the Subcommittee on Sea Power and Force Projection of the Committee on Armed Services*, 97th Cong., 1st sess., 1981, pt. 4:89.

157. Statement of F. Trubee Davison in "U.S. President's Air Policy Commission," unclassified testimony before the President's Air Policy Commission (Washington, DC [or D.C.]: 1 December 1947, mimeographed), 6:2644–49.

158. Davison, "U.S. President's Air Policy Commission," 6:2648. [shortened form]

Diaries, Minutes, Chronologies, Summaries, Digests, Notes, and So Forth

159. Diary of Fleet Adm William D. Leahy, 8 February 1946, William D. Leahy Papers, Manuscript Division, Library of Congress, Washington, DC [or D.C.].

160. Minutes of the War Department Board of Ordnance and Fortification, 24 October 1905, quoted in *Jones Aviation Chronology, 1900–1906*, 61.

161. Minutes of monthly meetings of Army Air Forces Board, 2 January 1945.

162. Minutes of the Patch Sword II Conference conducted at Headquarters AFSC, Andrews AFB, MD [or Md.], October 1981, 26.

163. Chronology, Astronautics and Aeronautics (NASA, 1966), 252, 305, 373.

164. Air Staff Summary Sheet, Lt Col Andrew C. Barbee, Policy and Plans Group, Report of Air Force Support of National Aeronautics and Space Administration, 20 March 1967.

165. Daily Staff Digest, Headquarters USAF, 13 November 1967.

166. Notes, Fifth Air Force Planning Conference, 12 December 1951.

167. Briefing, 6127th Air Terminal Group, subject: Air Terminal Detachments in Korea, 1 March 1951.

168. Brig Gen Mervin E. Gross, chief, Requirements Division, Aviation Section, Signal Corps, Office of the Chief of Research, Army Air Forces, record and routing (R&R) sheet, subject: Centralization of Certain Literature-Producing Functions at Orlando, FL [or Fla.], 27 November 1944.

169. Gross, R&R sheet. [shortened form]

170. FM 90-14, "Rear Battle," final draft, 19 November 1984, i.

Lectures and Addresses

171. Maj Gen Mason M. Patrick, "The Army Air Service" (lecture, Army War College, Carlisle Barracks, PA [or Pa.], 9 November 1925).

172. Patrick, "Army Air Service." [shortened form]

173. Gen Curtis E. LeMay, chief of staff, US Air Force (address, Air Force Association Convention, Philadelphia, PA [or Pa.], 21 September 1961).

174. Gen Earle G. Wheeler (graduation address, Industrial College of the Armed Forces, Washington, DC [or D.C.], 11 June 1963).

175. Sir Robert Saundby, "British Air Doctrine" (lecture, Air War College, Maxwell AFB, AL [or Ala.], 10 November 1953).

Interviews

176. Jerry Gibson (MCI Communications Corp.), interview by the author, 7 March 1983.

177. Gerald Sorbet (vice president, Fred's Frozen Foods, Bismarck, ND [or N. Dak.]), in discussion with the author, 21 October 2003.

178. Richard Voit, Warren Brasselle, and Kerry Deimer, interview by the author during visit to MCI Communications Corp., Southern Region, Atlanta, GA [or Ga.], 22 April 1983.

179. Maj Gen C. E. McKnight Jr. (US Army Communications Command, Fort Huachuca, AZ [or Ariz.]), interview by the author, 24 February 1983.

180. McKnight, interview. [shortened form]

181. Sorbet, discussion. [shortened form]

182. Lt Col Jerry A. Singleton, interview by Dr. James C. Hasdorff, 30 October 1992, transcript, 24, US Air Force Academy Library, Colorado Springs, CO [or Colo.].

183. McGeorge Bundy, interview by Robert MacNeil, *MacNeil/Lehrer NewsHour*, PBS, 7 February 1990.

184. Interview with colonel from Air Combat Command, 7 February 2004. (unattributed interview)

Video Recordings

185. Morris Massey, *What You Are Is*, CBS-Fox Video, 30 min., 1983, videocassette.

186. Louis J. Mihalyi, *Landscapes of Zambia, Central Africa* (Santa Barbara, CA [or Calif.]: Visual Education, 1975), slides.

Translation Services

187. Sergey Agafonov, "Japan in Russia's Financial Market: Bank of Tokyo to Open in Moscow," *Izvestiya*, 9 June 1992, 7, in *FBIS [Foreign Broadcast Information Service] Report: Central Eurasia*, FBIS-USR-92-079, 29 June 1992, 4.

188. A. Boldinyuk, "The Karelian Issue: Does It Exist, and If So, in What Form?" *Pravda*, 11 June 1992, 3, in FBIS-USR-92-079, 2. [subsequent reference to same FBIS issue]

189. Robert Minasov, "Gosznak Is Not Equal to the Task," *Rossiyskaya Gazeta*, 18 June 1992, 1, in FBIS-USR-92-080, 1 July 1992, 6. [subsequent reference to different FBIS issue but same coverage (i.e., Central Eurasia)]

190. "Opposition Parties Oppose Election Postponement," *Korea Times*, 25 June 1992, 2, in *FBIS Daily Report: East Asia*, FBIS-EAS-92-123, 25 June 1992, 23.

Electronic Publications

Electronic books

When citing electronic books available online, include as much of the information as can be determined that would also apply to printed books (author, title, volume, publisher, and so forth). Include the URL as part of the citation. You need not include the date accessed unless the material is particularly time-sensitive.

191. Col Richard T. Reynolds, *Heart of the Storm: The Genesis of the Air Campaign against Iraq* (Maxwell AFB, AL [or Ala.]: Air University Press, 1995), 19, http://aupress.maxwell.af.mil/Books/b-55/heartstm.pdf.

192. J. Sirosh, R. Miikkulainen, and J. A. Bednar, "Self-Organization of Orientation Maps, Lateral Connections, and Dynamic Fields in the Primary Visual Cortex," in *Lateral Interactions in the Cortex: Structure and Function*, ed. J. Sirosh, R. Miikkulainen, and Y. Choe (Austin, TX [or Tex.]: UTCS Neural Networks Research Group, 1996), http://www.cs.utexas.edu/users/nn/web-pubs/htmlbook96/ (accessed 27 August 2001). (*Chicago*, 17.143)

If you think it might be helpful to readers, you may indicate that a work is also available in forms other than the printed one:

193. Philip B. Kurland and Ralph Lerner, eds., *The Founders' Constitution* (Chicago: University of Chicago Press, 1987), also available online at http://press-pubs.uchicago.edu/founders/ and as a CD-ROM. (*Chicago*, 17.144)

Identify the format of non-Internet sources:

194. Thomas H. Davenport and John C. Beck, *The Attention Economy: Understanding the New Currency of Business* (Harvard Business School Press, 2001), TK3 Reader e-book. (*Chicago*, 17.145)

195. R. J. Hicks, *Nuclear Medicine, from the Center of Our Universe* (Victoria, Austl.: ICE T Multimedia, 1996), CD-ROM. (*Chicago*, 17.145)

Electronic journals

When citing electronic journals available online, include as much of the information as can be determined that would also apply to the printed version (author, title of article, volume, issue number, date, and so forth). Include the URL as part of the citation. You need not include the date accessed unless the material is particularly time-sensitive. Include specific page numbers if available; if not, add a descriptive locator (such as "The Consequences of Fear" in note 196 below) if you think it would be helpful to readers.

196. Gen Richard B. Myers, "A Word from the Chairman: Shift to a Global Perspective," *Air and Space Power Journal* 17, no. 3 (Fall 2003): 5, http://www
.airpower.maxwell.af.mil/airchronicles/apj/apj03/fal03/fal03.pdf.

197. Mark Warr and Christopher G. Ellison, "Rethinking Social Reactions to Crime: Personal and Altruistic Fear in Family Households," *American Journal of Sociology* 106, no. 3 (2000), under "The Consequences of Fear," http://www.journals.uchicago.edu/AJS/journal/issues/v106n3/050125.html. (*Chicago*, 17.181)

Online magazines

When citing online magazines, include as much of the information as can be determined that would also apply to the printed version (author, title of article, date, and so forth). Include the URL as part of the citation. You need not include the date accessed unless the material is particularly time-sensitive. Include specific page numbers if available.

198. Jessica Reaves, "A Weighty Issue: Ever-Fatter Kids," interview with James Rosen, *Time*, 14 March 2001, http://www.time.com/time/nation/article/0,8599,102443,00.html. (*Chicago*, 17.187)

199. Lawrence Osborne, "Poison Pen," review of *The Collaborator: The Trial and Execution of Robert Brasillach*, by Alice Kaplan, *Salon*, 29 March 2000, http://www.salon.com/books/it/2000/03/29/kaplan/index.html (accessed 10 July 2001). (*Chicago*, 17.187)

Online newspapers, news services, and other news sites

When citing online newspapers or news articles posted by news services, include as much of the information as can be determined that would also apply to the printed version (author, title of article, date, and so forth). Include the URL as part of the citation. You need not include the date accessed unless the material is particularly time-sensitive.

200. Alison Mitchell and Frank Bruni, "Scars Still Raw, Bush Clashes with McCain," *New York Times*, 25 March 2001, http://www.nytimes.com/2001/03/25/politics/25MCCA.html (accessed 2 January 2002). (*Chicago*, 17.198)

201. Richard Stenger, "Tiny Human-Borne Monitoring Device Sparks Privacy Fears," *CNN.com*, 20 December 1999, http://www.cnn.com/1999/TECH/ptech/12/20/implant.device/. (*Chicago*, 17.198)

If a URL has become invalid before publication of the work in which it is cited or if the article comes from an online source for a fee, include only the address of the "home page" (note that such URLs end with a slash, as do other directory-level URLs) (Chicago, 17.198).

202. Reuters, "Russian Blasts Kill 21, Injure More Than 140," *Yahoo! News*, 24 March 2001, http://dailynews.yahoo.com/. (*Chicago*, 17.198)

Electronic mailing lists

To cite material from an electronic mailing list that has been archived online, include the name of the list, date of the individual posting, and the URL. You need not include the date accessed unless the material is particularly time-sensitive. (*Chicago*, 17.236)

203. John Powell, e-mail to Grapevine mailing list, 23 April 1998, http://www.electriceditors.net/grapevine/issues/83.txt. (*Chicago*, 17.236)

Site content

For original content from online sources other than periodicals, include as much of the following as can be determined: author of the content, title of the page, title or owner of the site, and URL. (Chicago, 17.237)

204. Evanston Public Library Board of Trustees, "Evanston Public Library Strategic Plan, 2000–2010: A Decade of Outreach," Evanston Public Library, http://www.epl.org/library/strategic-plan-oo.html (accessed 18 July 2002). (*Chicago*, 17.237)

If there is no author, you may substitute the owner of the site (Chicago, 17.237):

205. Federation of American Scientists, "Resolution Comparison: Reading License Plates and Headlines," http://www.fas.org/irp/imint/resolve5.htm. (*Chicago*, 17.237)

Since very informal sites, such as personal home pages and fan sites, may have no titles, you may use descriptive phrases (Chicago, 17.237):

206. Camp Taconic Alumni, 1955 photo gallery, http://www.taconicalumni.org/1955.html. (*Chicago*, 17.237)
207. Pete Townshend's official Web site, "Biography," http://www.petetownshend.co.uk/petet_bio.html. (*Chicago*, 17.237)

If a site ceases to exist before publication of the work in which it is cited, say so parenthetically at the end of the citation, separated from the access date, if any, by a semicolon (Chicago, 17.237):

208. Pete Townshend's official Web site, "Biography," http://www.petetownshend.co.uk/petet_bio.html (accessed 15 December 2001; site now discontinued). (*Chicago*, 17.237)

Reference works online

When citing online versions of encyclopedias and dictionaries, follow the format for the printed versions (see above) and always include an access date in addition to the URL. Sometimes it may be appropriate to include the author of an entry (Chicago, 17.239).

209. *Encyclopaedia Britannica Online*, s.v. "Sibelius, Jean," http://search.eb.com/bol/topic?eu=69347&sctn=1 (accessed 3 January 2002). (*Chicago*, 17.239)

210. *The New Grove Dictionary of Music and Musicians*, s.v. "Sibelius, Jean" (by James Hepokoski), http://www.grovemusic.com/ (accessed 3 January 2002). (*Chicago*, 17.239)

Online multimedia

When citing online multimedia, include such information as the name of the composer, writer, performer, or person responsible for the content; the title, in italics; the name of the recording company or publisher; the identifying number of the recording; the URL; and the type of medium. You need not include the date accessed unless the material is particularly time-sensitive (Chicago, 17.266, 17.270).

211. A. E. Weed, *At the Foot of the Flatiron* (American Mutoscope and Biograph Co., 1903), 2 min., 19 sec.; 35 mm; from Library of Congress, *The Life of a City: Early Films of New York, 1898–1906*, MPEG, http://lcweb2.loc.gov/ammem/papr/nychome.html (accessed 14 August 2001). (*Chicago*, 17.270)

In the following note, the audiovisual material is associated with a specific article in an electronic journal (Chicago, 17.270):

212. *Naraya* no. 2, "Ghost Dancing Music" (MP3 audio file), Richard W. Stoffle, Lawrence Loendorf, Diane E. Austin, David B. Halmo, and Angelita Bulletts, "Ghost Dancing the Grand Canyon," *Current Anthropology* 41, no. 1 (2000), http://www. journals.uchicago.edu/CA/journal/issues/v41n1/001001/001001.html. (*Chicago*, 17.270)

CD-ROM or DVD-ROM

Citations to works issued on CD-ROM are similar to those for printed works. You may omit place of publication and date unless they are relevant (Chicago, 17.271).

213. *Complete National Geographic: 110 Years of National Geographic Magazine*, CD-ROM, Mindscape, 2000. (*Chicago*, 17.271)
214. *Oxford English Dictionary*, 2nd ed., CD-ROM, version 2.0, Oxford University Press. (*Chicago*, 17.271)

Public documents online

When citing online public documents, follow the format for printed materials (see above), adding a URL and, if necessary, an access date (Chicago, 17.356).

215. Illinois Constitution, art. 2, sec. 2, http://www.legis.state.il.us/ commission/lrb/conmain.htm. (*Chicago*, 17.356)
216. US Census Bureau, "Health Insurance Coverage Status and Type of Coverage by Sex, Race, and Hispanic Origin, 1987 to 1999," Health Insurance Historical Table 1, 2000, http://www.census.gov/hhes/hlthins/ historic/hihistt.html. (*Chicago*, 17.356)
217. L. A. Adamic and B. A. Huberman, "The Nature of Markets in the World Wide Web," working paper (Xerox Palo Alto Research Center, 1999), http://www.parc.xerox.com/istl/groups/iea/www/webmarkets.html (accessed 1 March 2001). (*Chicago*, 17.356)

APPENDIX B

Bibliographic Entries

Examples of several categories of bibliographic citations appear below. For other examples, see the entry *bibliography* (5.2) and page 181 in this guide, as well as the 15th edition of *The Chicago Manual of Style*.

Books

One author

Westmoreland, Gen William C. *A Soldier Reports*. Garden City, NY [or N.Y.]: Doubleday & Co., 1976.

Two authors

Masland, John W., and Laurence I. Radway. *Soldiers and Scholars: Military Education and National Policy*. Princeton, NJ [or N.J.]: Princeton University Press, 1957.

Three authors

Strausz-Hupe, Robert, William R. Kintner, and Stefan T. Possony. *A Forward Strategy for America*. New York: Harper & Bros., 1961.

More than three authors

Pomper, Gerald, William G. Mayer, Marjorie Randon Hershey, and Kathleen A. Frankovic. *The Election of 1976*. New York: McKay, 1977. [For four to 10 authors or editors, include all names.]

No author given

Soviet Military Power. Washington, DC [or D.C.]: Government Printing Office, 1983.

Editor, compiler, or translator

Clausewitz, Carl von. *On War*. Edited and translated by Michael Howard and Peter Paret. Princeton, NJ [or N.J.]: Princeton University Press, 1976.

Goldberg, Alfred, ed. *A History of the United States Air Force, 1907–1957*. Princeton, NJ [or N.J.]: D. Van Nostrand, 1957.

Mayer, J. P. *Alexis de Tocqueville: Democracy in America*. Translated by George Lawrence. New York: Doubleday & Co., 1969.

Multivolume works and series

Craven, Wesley Frank, and James Lea Cate, eds. *The Army Air Forces in World War II.* 7 vols. 1948–1958. New imprint, Washington, D.C.: Office of Air Force History, 1983.

————. *The Army Air Forces in World War II.* Vol. 2, *Europe: Torch to Pointblank, August 1942 to December 1943.* 1949. New imprint, Washington, D.C.: Office of Air Force History, 1983.

Trest, Warren A. *Military Unity and National Policy: Some Past Effects and Future Implications.* CADRE Paper Special Series: The Future of the Air Force, no. AU-ARI-CPSS-91-7. Maxwell AFB, AL [or Ala.]: Air University Press, December 1991.

Association or institution as author

Gates Commission. *The Report of the President's Commission on an All-Volunteer Armed Force.* Washington, DC [or D.C.]: Government Printing Office, 1970.

Work of one author in a work edited by another

Warden, Col John A., III. "Air Theory for the Twenty-first Century." In *Challenge and Response: Anticipating US Military Security Concerns,* edited by Dr. Karl P. Magyar, Lt Col Maris McCrabb, Lt Col Albert U. Mitchum Jr., and Dr. Lewis B. Ware, 351–75. Maxwell AFB, AL [or Ala.]: Air University Press, August 1994.

Edition

Hazard, John N. *The Soviet System of Government.* 5th ed. Chicago: University of Chicago Press, 1980.

Reprint editions

Harris, Neil. *The Artist in American Society: The Formative Years, 1790–1860.* 1966. Reprint, Chicago: University of Chicago Press, 1982.

Periodicals

Volume number not shown

"Congress Sends Nixon a Message." *Newsweek,* 19 November 1973, 39.

Volume number shown

Rosser, Col Richard F. "American Civil-Military Relations in the 1980s." *Naval War College Review* 24, no. 10 (June 1972): [first and last page numbers of article (e.g., 14–20)].

Newspaper Items

Newspapers are more commonly cited in notes or parenthetical references than in bibliographies (Chicago, 17.191). However, if you wish to include a bibliographic entry, use the following format:

Konz, Antoinette. "District Results Released." *Montgomery Advertiser*, 11 August 2005.

Encyclopedia Articles

Well-known reference books are usually not listed in bibliographies.

Historical Studies

Finney, Robert T. *History of the Air Corps Tactical School, 1920–1940.* USAF Historical Study 100. Maxwell AFB, AL [or Ala.]: USAF Historical Division, Air University, 1955.

Staff Studies

Evaluation Division, Air University. To Analyze the USAF Publications System for Producing Manuals. Staff study, 13 July 1948.

Staudenmaier, Col Herbert V. CONUS Aeromedical Evacuation Study. Staff study, 31 March 1983.

Unit and Staff Office Histories

History. Deputy Chief of Staff for Plans and Programs, Directorate of Plans, Headquarters USAF, July–December 1958.

History. Tactical Air Command, 1 July–31 December 1953.

Reports

Published

Erickson, John. *The Soviet Military, Soviet Policy, and Soviet Politics.* USSI Report 73-3. Washington, DC [or D.C.]: United States Strategic Institute, 1973.

Management of Internet Names and Addresses. US Government White Paper. Washington, DC [or D.C.]: Department of Commerce, June 1998.

Unpublished

Hungerford, Maj John B., Jr. "Organization for Military Space: A Historical Perspective." Research Report no. 82-1235. Maxwell AFB, AL [or Ala.]: Air Command and Staff College, 1982.

Unpublished Papers

Betts, Richard K. "Soldiers, Statesmen, and Resort to Force: American Military Influence in Crisis Decisions, 1945–1976." PhD diss., Harvard University, 1975.

Ross, Dorothy. "The Irish-Catholic Immigrant, 1880–1900: A Study in Social Mobility." Master's thesis, Columbia University, n.d.

Thomas, P. "Utilization of Enlisted Women in the Military." Paper presented at the RAND Conference on Defense Manpower. Santa Monica, CA [or Calif.], February 1976.

Manuscript Collections

Dinkel, Joseph. Description of Louis Agassiz written at the request of Elizabeth Cary Agassiz. Agassiz Papers. Houghton Library, Harvard University.

Egmont Manuscripts. Phillipps Collection. University of Georgia Library. [Specific items are not included in a bibliography unless only one item from a collection is cited.]

House, Edward M. Papers. Yale University Library.

Johnson, Alvin. Memorandum, 1937. File 36. Horace Kallen Papers. YIVO Institute, New York.

Legal Citations

AT&T Corporation v. Iowa Utilities. In *United States Supreme Court Reports*. Vol. 525, 1999.

Lugosi v. Universal. In *California Reports*. 3d [or 3rd] series. Vol. 25. California Supreme Court, 1976.

Public Documents

Bills, reports, and miscellaneous documents

US House. *A Bill to Require Passenger-Carrying Motor Vehicles Purchased for Use by the Federal Government to Meet Certain Safety Standards.* 86th Cong., 1st sess., 1959. H. R. 1341.

US Senate. *Documents on the International Aspects of the Exploration and Use of Outer Space, 1954–1962.* 88th Cong., 1st sess., 1963. S. Doc. 18.

US Senate. *Report of the Federal Trade Commission on Utility Corporations.* 70th Cong., 1st sess., 1935. S. Doc. 92.

Hearings

US Senate. *Study of Air Power: Hearings before the Subcommittee on the Air Force of the Committee on Armed Services.* 84th Cong., 2d [or 2nd] sess., 1956.

Congressional bills and resolutions

Atomic Energy Act of 1946. Public Law 585. 79th Cong., 2d [or 2nd] sess., 1 August 1946.

Atomic Energy Act of 1946. US Statutes at Large 60 (1947): 755–75.

Declaratory Judgment Act. US Code. Vol. 28, secs. 2201–2 (1952).

US House. *Food Security Act of 1985.* 99th Cong., 1st sess., H. R. 2100. *Congressional Record,* 131, no. 132, daily ed. (8 October 1985): H8461–66.

Executive department documents

US Department of Defense. *Profile of American Youth: 1980 Administration of the Armed Services Vocational Aptitude Battery.* Washington, DC [or D.C.]: Office of the Assistant Secretary of Defense (Manpower, Reserve Affairs and Logistics), March 1982.

Presidential proclamations, executive orders, other documents

Eisenhower, Dwight D. *Public Papers of the Presidents of the United States: Dwight D. Eisenhower, 1957.* Washington, DC [or D.C.]: Government Printing Office, 1958.

Executive Order 9877. Functions of the Armed Services, 26 July 1947.

President. Proclamation. "Supplemental Quota on Imports of Long-Staple Cotton." *Federal Register* 15, no. 196 (10 October 1950): 127. Microfiche.

Classified Sources

Assistant Chief of Staff, Intelligence. "Linebacker II: 18–29 December 72" (U). Supporting document III-K1. (Top Secret) Information extracted is unclassified.

Faloon, Robert L. *Strategic Air Defense in Nuclear War* (U). Maxwell AFB, AL [or Ala.]: Air University Press, 1983. (Secret) Information extracted is unclassified.

TAF SON 302-81. *Statement of Operational Need for Night Attack Capabilities* (U), 2 November 1982. (Secret)

Declassified Sources

Central Intelligence Agency. *National Intelligence Estimate Number 11-5-57.* Washington, DC [or D.C.]: Central Intelligence Agency, 1957. Document is now declassified.

Letters, E-Mails, and Indorsements

Culver, Lt Col C. C. To chief of Air Corps. Letter, 9 June 1928. 1st ind. Maj L. W. McIntosh, executive, Office of the Chief of Air Corps. To commandant, Air Corps Tactical School, 1 September 1928.

Kilner, Maj W. G., executive, Office of Chief of Air Service. To commandant, Air Service Tactical School. Letter, 12 April 1925.

Smith, Maj John, chief, Office of Public Affairs, Maxwell AFB, AL. To the author. E-mail, 20 November 2005.

Memorandums

Regular memorandum

Bundy, Lt Col G. W. War Plans Division, War Department General Staff. To Lt Col Clayton J. Bissell, War Plans Division. Memorandum, 18 July 1941.

Draft memorandum

Chief, Air Corps. To chief of staff, Army. Draft memorandum, 28 March 1938.

Memorandum of understanding

Secretary of the Army. To secretary of the Air Force. Memorandum of understanding, 2 October 1951.

Memorandum for record

Twining, Gen Nathan F., vice-chief of staff, US Air Force. Memorandum for record, 17 November 1950.

Messages

Message. 281415Z OCT 90. US Air Force. To commanding general, Far East
Air Forces, 28 October 1990.

Manuals, Instructions, Directives,
and Other Publications

Air Force Doctrine Document (AFDD) 1. *Air Force Basic Doctrine*, 17
November 2003.
Air Force Instruction (AFI) 90-901. *Operational Risk Management*, 1 April
2000.
Air Force Manual (AFMAN) 36-505. *Skill Coding*, 1 August 1996.
Air Force Pamphlet (AFPAM) 36-106. *Supervisor's Records*, 20 December
1993.
Department of Defense (DOD) Directive 5015.2. *DOD Records Management
Program*, 6 March 2000.

Sources Cited/Quoted in Another Source

McNamara, Robert, secretary of defense. To Cong. Robert Miller. Letter, 3
November 1961. In US House. *Sundry Legislation Affecting the Naval
and Military Establishment, 1963: Hearings before the Committee on
Armed Services.* 88th Cong., 1st sess., 1963.

Diaries, Minutes, Chronologies,
Summaries, Digests, Notes, and So Forth

Barbee, Lt Col Andrew C., Policy and Plans Group. Air Staff Summary Sheet.
Report of Air Force Support of National Aeronautics and Space Ad-
ministration, 20 March 1967.
Briefing. 6127th Air Terminal Group. Subject: Air Terminal Detachments in
Korea, 1 March 1951.
Chronology. Astronautics and Aeronautics (NASA, 1966).
Daily Staff Digest. Headquarters USAF, 13 November 1967.
Field Manual (FM) 90-14. "Rear Battle." Final draft, 19 November 1984.
Gross, Brig Gen Mervin E., chief, Requirements Division, Aviation Section,
Signal Corps, Office of the Chief of Research, Army Air Forces. Record
and Routing (R&R) sheet. Subject: Centralization of Certain Literature-
Producing Functions at Orlando, FL [or Fla.], 27 November 1944.

Leahy, Fleet Adm William D. Diary. William D. Leahy Papers. Manuscript Division, Library of Congress, Washington, DC [or D.C.].
Minutes. War Department Board of Ordnance and Fortification, 24 October 1905. In *Jones Aviation Chronology, 1900–1906.*
Notes. Fifth Air Force Planning Conference, 12 December 1951.

Lectures and Addresses

LeMay, Gen Curtis E., chief of staff, US Air Force. Address. Air Force Association Convention, Philadelphia, PA [or Pa.], 21 September 1961.
Patrick, Maj Gen Mason M. "The Army Air Service." Lecture. Army War College, Carlisle Barracks, PA [or Pa.], 9 November 1925.
Wheeler, Gen Earle G. Graduation address. Industrial College of the Armed Forces, Washington, DC [or D.C.], 11 June 1963.

Interviews

It is not necessary to include interviews in a bibliography. You may wish to include a transcript of an interview, however.

Video Recordings

Massey, Morris. *What You Are Is.* CBS-Fox Video. 30 min., 1983. Video-cassette.
Mihalyi, Louis J. *Landscapes of Zambia, Central Africa.* Santa Barbara, CA [or Calif.]: Visual Education, 1975. Slides.

Translation Services

Agafonov, Sergey. "Japan in Russia's Financial Market: Bank of Tokyo to Open in Moscow." *Izvestiya,* 9 June 1992. In *FBIS [Foreign Broadcast Information Service] Report: Central Eurasia.* FBIS-USR-92-079, 29 June 1992.

Electronic Publications

Electronic books

Davenport, Thomas H., and John C. Beck. *The Attention Economy: Understanding the New Currency of Business.* Harvard Business School Press, 2001. TK3 Reader e-book.

Hicks, R. J. *Nuclear Medicine, from the Center of Our Universe.* Victoria, Austl.: ICE T Multimedia, 1996. CD-ROM.

Sirosh, J., R. Miikkulainen, and J. A. Bednar. "Self-Organization of Orientation Maps, Lateral Connections, and Dynamic Fields in the Primary Visual Cortex." In *Lateral Interactions in the Cortex: Structure and Function,* ed. J. Sirosh, R. Miikkulainen, and Y. Choe. Austin, TX [or Tex.]: UTCS Neural Networks Research Group, 1996. http://www.cs.utexas.edu/users/ nn/web-pubs/htmlbook96/ (accessed 27 August 2001).

Electronic journals

Myers, Gen Richard B. "A Word from the Chairman: Shift to a Global Perspective." *Air and Space Power Journal* 17, no. 3 (Fall 2003): 5–10. http://www.airpower.maxwell.af.mil/airchronicles/apj/apj03/fal03/fal03 .pdf (accessed 29 September 2003).

Online magazines

Reaves, Jessica. "A Weighty Issue: Ever-Fatter Kids." Interview with James Rosen. *Time,* 14 March 2001. http://www.time.com/time/ nation/article/0,8599,102443,00.html.

Online newspapers, news services, and other news sites

Mitchell, Alison, and Frank Bruni. "Scars Still Raw, Bush Clashes with McCain." *New York Times,* 25 March 2001. http://www.nytimes.com/ 2001/03/25/politics/25MCCA.html (accessed 2 January 2002).

Reuters. "Russian Blasts Kill 21, Injure More Than 140." *Yahoo! News,* 24 March 2001. http://dailynews.yahoo.com/.

Stenger, Richard. "Tiny Human-Borne Monitoring Device Sparks Privacy Fears." *CNN.com,* 20 December 1999. http://www.cnn.com/1999/TECH/ ptech/12/20/implant.device/.

Electronic mailing lists

Powell, John. E-mail to Grapevine mailing list, 23 April 1998. http://www .electriceditors.net/grapevine/issues/83.txt.

Site content

Evanston Public Library Board of Trustees. "Evanston Public Library Strategic Plan, 2000–2010: A Decade of Outreach." Evanston Public Library. http://www.epl.org/library/strategic-plan-oo.html (accessed 18 July 2002).

Federation of American Scientists. "Resolution Comparison: Reading License Plates and Headlines." http://www.fas.org/irp/imint/resolve5.htm.

Pete Townshend's official Web site. "Biography." http: //www.petetownshend
.co.uk/petet_bio.html.

Online multimedia

Weed, A. E. *At the Foot of the Flatiron.* American Mutoscope and Biograph
Co., 1903; 2 min., 19 sec.; 35 mm. From Library of Congress, *The Life of
a City: Early Films of New York, 1898–1906.* MPEG. http:// lcweb2.loc
.gov/ammem/papr/nychome.html (accessed 14 August 2001).

CD-ROM or DVD-ROM

Complete National Geographic: 110 Years of National Geographic Magazine.
CD-ROM. Mindscape, 2000.
Oxford English Dictionary. 2nd ed. CD-ROM, version 2.0. Oxford University
Press.

Public documents online

Adamic, L. A., and B. A. Huberman. "The Nature of Markets in the World
Wide Web." Working paper. Xerox Palo Alto Research Center, 1999.
http://www.parc.xerox.com/istl/groups/iea/www/webmarkets.html
(accessed 1 March 2001).
Illinois Constitution, art. 2, sec. 2. http://www.legis.state.il.us/commission/lrb/
conmain.htm.
US Census Bureau. "Health Insurance Coverage Status and Type of Coverage
by Sex, Race, and Hispanic Origin, 1987 to 1999." Health Insurance
Historical Table 1, 2000. http://www.census.gov/hhes/hlthins/historic/
hihistt.html.

APPENDIX C

Copyright

An "original work of authorship" is protected by the copyright laws of the United States, regardless of whether the work is published and whether it is registered with the United States Copyright Office (a department of the Library of Congress). "Works of authorship" include written manuscripts and other literary works, as well as original graphic or pictorial material, visual art, audiovisual works, motion pictures, and sound recordings. The owner of a copyright has exclusive rights of reproduction, adaptation, publication, performance, and display of the work (if the work is to be published, he or she may transfer some or all of these rights to the publisher by formal agreement). For that reason, if you intend to use another person's work (e.g., text, graphs, tables, photographs, paintings, film clips, music clips, etc.) in a work of your own, you must obtain written permission from the copyright owner, whether individual or publisher. Two important exceptions to this principle follow.

First, you need not obtain permission if the work is in the public domain. Such works are considered public property and may be used by anybody. A work of the United States government (defined as a work prepared by an officer or employee of the United States government as part of that person's official duties) is in the public domain, as is a work whose copyright has expired. *Effective January 1, 1978, the Copyright Act of 1976 provided that duration of a copyright is the life of the author plus 70 years. In the case of a "work made for hire," the law regards the employer or other controlling party as the "author" and provides a term of 95 years from the date of publication or 120 years from the date of creation, whichever is shorter, for the duration of copyright. When the author is unknown or has published under a pseudonym, the same length of time applies as for a work made for hire (95 years from the date of publication or 120 years from the date of creation). If, after publication, the author's name is revealed and recorded with the Copyright Office, the "life plus 70" principle takes over (unless the work was made for hire). For unpublished works under the old copyright law (prior to 1978), their copyright extends at least to December 31, 2002. If they were published before that date, protection lasts until December 31, 2047, giving them a term of 70 years from the date the new law went into effect and longer if the authors' lives extended beyond 1977. Works published before December 31, 1922, are in the public domain. Works published from 1923 through 1963 are still protected if their copyright was renewed in the 28th year after first publication. The renewal term for these works is now 67 years rather than 28, but if no initial registration or renewal was properly filed, they are in the public domain. Works published from 1964 through 1977 are protected for 95 years from first publication. If you have any doubts about the currency of a work's copyright, check with the Copyright Office* (Chicago, 4.9, 4.22–.26).

Second, you need not obtain permission if you use material in accordance with the doctrine of fair use. This doctrine allows you to use another person's work for purposes of criticism, comment, news reporting, teaching, scholarship, or research. For example, you may quote passages of copyrighted material for purposes of critical analysis and review or for purposes of supporting your own work. You may also reproduce copyrighted pictorial material for critical purposes (e.g., use of a photograph to facilitate commentary on techniques of photographic composition). In determining whether a use is fair, the doctrine considers the following four factors:

1. *The purpose and character of the use, including whether such use is of a commercial nature or is for nonprofit educational purposes.* Commercial use generally is presumed to be unfair. On the other hand, nonprofit educational use is not deemed automatically to be fair, but it is more likely to be so treated, particularly if a public benefit results from the use.
2. *The nature of the copyrighted work.* The use of creative works, as opposed to informational ones, is less likely to be deemed fair use. Fictional works are afforded more protection than factual ones.
3. *The amount and substantiality of the portion used in relation to the copyrighted work as a whole.* The doctrine of fair use does not specify a particular number of words, lines, graphs, and so forth, that you may use without permission. A rule of reasonableness applies, both quantitatively and qualitatively. Generally speaking, you cannot reproduce a work in its entirety—a poem, an essay, a song, or an individually copyrighted article in a journal or magazine—without obtaining permission. Nor can you use the "heart of the work" (i.e., the key or essential material) without obtaining permission.
4. *The effect of the use upon the potential market for, or value of, the copyrighted work.* While all of the factors must be considered in determining the applicability of the fair-use doctrine, this fourth and final factor is the single most important element of the analysis. Commercial use is presumptively harmful to the future value of the work used. Noncommercial use, however, requires a meaningful (and demonstrable) likelihood of future harm before the use is considered unfair.

Whether or not you obtain permission from the copyright owner to use part of a work, you should always credit the author and the source of the borrowed material (see also plagiarism [5.6]). Merely acknowledging the source does not substitute for obtaining permission if circumstances so dictate. If you do obtain permission, you should identify your source, followed by a statement such as "Reprinted by permission of the publisher." An illustration should be accompanied by a note such as "Courtesy of the Metropolitan Museum of Art."

The rapid expansion of electronic communications and the growth of the Internet have given rise to complex legal issues that are as yet unresolved. Pending legislation and ongoing litigation will no doubt have an effect on how copyright laws are applied online. In the meantime, you would do well to assume that the same principles of copyright protection that apply to traditional written and pictorial material also apply to materials found online. That is, you should obtain permission to use any text, photographs, artwork, and so forth that you find online unless that material is in the public domain or you reproduce it in accordance with the doctrine of fair use (and you should credit your source in any case). Likewise, you should apply the same principles that apply to materials you use in your printed writings to any materials you want to use in electronic or multimedia creations, such as CD-ROM or DVD-ROM.

Bibliography

Air War College. *Handbook on Research and Writing.* Maxwell AFB, AL [or Ala.]: Air University, 1982.

AU-12. *Plain English, Please!* Prepared by John Smith and Maj John R. Grellman Jr. Maxwell AFB, AL [or Ala.]: Air University, 1982.

The Chicago Manual of Style. 15th ed. Chicago: University of Chicago Press, 2003.

Copperud, Roy H. *American Usage and Style: The Consensus.* New York: Van Nostrand Reinhold Co., 1980.

Ebbitt, Wilma R., and David R. Ebbitt. *Index to English.* 8th ed. Oxford: Oxford University Press, 1990.

Evans, Bergen, and Cornelia Evans. *A Dictionary of Contemporary American Usage.* New York: Random House, 1957.

Gibaldi, Joseph. *MLA Handbook for Writers of Research Papers.* New York: Modern Language Association of America, 1999.

Heflin, Woodford Agee, ed. *The United States Air Force Dictionary.* Maxwell AFB, AL [or Ala.]: Air University Press, 1956.

The Merriam-Webster Dictionary of English Usage. Springfield, MA [or Mass.]: Merriam-Webster, Inc., 1989.

Merriam-Webster's Collegiate Dictionary. 11th ed. Springfield, MA [or Mass.]: Merriam-Webster, Inc., 2003.

Siegal, Allan M. *The New York Times Manual of Style and Usage.* New York: Times Books, 1999.

Turabian, Kate L. *A Manual for Writers of Term Papers, Theses, and Dissertations.* 6th ed. Chicago: University of Chicago Press, 1996.

United States Government Printing Office: Style Manual. Washington, DC [or D.C.]: Government Printing Office, 1984.

Webster's Third New International Dictionary of the English Language, Unabridged. Springfield, MA [or Mass.]: G. & C. Merriam Co., 1981.

Index

ISR (intelligence, surveillance, and reconnaissance), 2.200
it, 3.1.10
italics, 4.4
IW (information warfare), 2.201
I&W (indications and warning), 2.202

J-1 (manpower and personnel directorate of
a joint staff), 2.203
J-2 (intelligence directorate of a joint staff),
2.204
J-3 (operations directorate of a joint staff),
2.205
J-4 (logistics directorate of a joint staff),
2.206
J-5 (plans directorate of a joint staff), 2.207
J-6 (command, control, communications,
and computer systems directorate of a
joint staff), 2.208
J-7 (Operational Plans and Joint Force
Development, Joint Staff), 2.209
J-8 (Director for Force Structure, Resource,
and Assessment, Joint Staff), 2.210
JAG (judge advocate general), 2.211
JAOC (joint air [and space] operations cen-
ter), 2.212
JAOP (joint air [and space] operations plan),
2.213
JASSM (Joint Air-to-Surface Standoff
Missile), 2.214
JCS (Joint Chiefs of Staff), 2.215
JDAM (Joint Direct Attack Munition),
2.216
jeep, 4.1.85
JFACC (joint force air [and space] compo-
nent commander), 2.217
JFC (joint force commander), 2.218
JFLCC (joint force land component com-
mander), 2.219
JFMCC (joint force maritime component
commander), 2.220
JFSOCC (joint force special operations com-
ponent commander), 2.221
JOC (joint operations center), 2.222
joint doctrine, 4.1.86
Joint Staff, 4.1.87
journals, 4.1.88, 4.4.9
JP (joint publication), 2.223

Jr., 2.224
JSOW (joint standoff weapon), 2.225
JSTARS (Joint Surveillance Target Attack
Radar System), 2.226
JTF (joint task force), 2.227
judicial branch, 4.1.89

-keeper, 4.2.135
kg (kilogram), 2.228
kHz (kilohertz), 2.229
KIA (killed in action), 2.230
km (kilometer), 2.231
Korean conflict, 4.1.90
Korean War, 4.1.91

landmass, 4.2.136
land power, 4.2.137
LANDSAT (land satellite), 2.232
LANTIRN (low-altitude navigation and targeting infrared for night), 2.233
latitude, 1.36, 2.234
laws, 4.1.4, 4.1.92
legal cases, 4.4.10
legend, 1.18
legislative bodies, 4.1.93
legislative branch, 4.1.93
LEO (low Earth orbit), 2.235
LF (low frequency), 2.236
LGB (laser-guided bomb), 2.237
LGM (laser-guided missile), 2.238
LGW (laser-guided weapon), 2.239
LIC (low intensity conflict), 2.240
LIMFAC (limiting factor), 2.241
lists, 1.37
LOC (line of communications), 2.242
localities, 4.1.94
loc. cit. *(loco citato)*, 2.243
log-in (n.), 4.2.139
log in (v.), 4.2.138
logistic or logistical, 4.2.140
logistics (n.), 3.1.12
log-off (n.), 4.2.142
log off (v.), 4.2.141
log-on (n.), 4.2.144
log on (v.), 4.2.143
longitude, 1.36, 2.234
long term (n.), 4.2.145
long-term (adj.), 4.2.146

Part 2

Air University Press Author Guide

About Us

Air University (AU) Press, a division of AU's Fairchild Library at Maxwell AFB, Alabama, publishes school-selected student papers, faculty research efforts, textbooks, and curriculum-related materials, as well as the *Air University Catalog* and other administrative documents that directly support AU's program of professional military education (PME). The series of school-sponsored papers we support include Air War College's Maxwell Papers, Air Command and Staff College's Wright Flyers, theses by students at the School of Advanced Air and Space Studies (SAASS), and the College of Aerospace Doctrine, Research and Education's (CADRE) Papers. AU Press itself sponsors the Fairchild Papers, selected essays having research value to the Air Force. Under the guidance of the AU Publication Review Board, at the instruction of higher-level headquarters, and in cooperation with Air Force agencies, we also publish monographs, books, and other research and educational materials, as well as the English, Spanish, Portuguese, Arabic, and French (forthcoming) editions of *Air and Space Power Journal*, the professional flagship journal of the Air Force.

Over the years, we have compiled a significant body of literature on how best to employ airpower. For information about these publications, used by airpower scholars and students throughout the world, please see our catalog, *Air University Press Publications*; to obtain copies, visit our bookstore at 131 West Shumacher Avenue, Maxwell AFB, AL 36112-6615 (telephone 334-953-2773, DSN 493-2773, or fax 334-953-6862) or browse our Web site: http://aupress.maxwell.af.mil. Our publications are also available from the US Government Printing Office (visit GPO's online bookstore at http://bookstore.gpo.gov).

Payment

If you are a government employee who has written a manuscript as part of your job; has used government time, equipment, supplies, or facilities to do so; or has composed a study based on knowledge gained through official duties, then government laws and regulations prohibit you from accepting payment for your work. In some cases, however, sponsoring agencies may commission manuscripts for publication by AU Press. In any case, we do not pay for the manuscripts we publish. If appropriate, payment is negotiated between an author and the sponsoring agency. You should also be aware that since AU Press is a government agency, its publications are not copyrighted but are in the public domain.

Classified Material

As a rule, AU Press does not process or publish classified material. If you (the author or the office of primary responsibility [OPR]) believe that your project merits an exception to this rule, please notify our director as early in the development process as possible. If a waiver is granted, you are responsible for providing downgrading/declassification instructions and for properly marking the entire manuscript (pages, paragraphs, endnotes, and illustrations in both the paper and disk copies) for compliance with security regulations. We will mark the published product in accordance with your or the security and policy review authority's instructions. The OPR is responsible for retaining record copies of the printed materials and arranging for their downgrading/declassification after the classification expires or as sensitive information is cleared for public release.

Security and Policy Review

The publications that we intend to release to the public must undergo security clearance and policy review by the public affairs (PA) office here at Maxwell to ensure that they contain no classified information and do not misrepresent current Air Force policy. We request this review as soon as your manuscript is approved for publication. We cannot edit or otherwise process your work until we receive clearance from the PA officer at Maxwell. If you wish, you may have your manuscript cleared by your local PA office.

Obviously, you should make sure that your manuscript contains no classified or sensitive information (e.g., inspector-general reports or other documents marked "For Official Use Only" [FOUO], Social Security numbers, etc.). If you cite unclassified material from a classified document, indicate that fact in an endnote, along with the overall classification of the document (e.g., [Secret] Information extracted is unclassified). Be advised that your manuscript may have to go through security review at either the Air Force or DOD level to certify that the extracted material is indeed unclassified.

Production Schedule

A number of variables affect our publication process (fig. 1). These include its length and quality, your availability to work with the editor, the workload and priorities of the press team assigned to your project, and the competence of the contract company selected to do the printing. Our experience suggests that the following schedule represents a reasonable estimate of the amount of time we require to publish your study:

- book   -   nine to 12 months
- Fairchild Paper   -   six months
- CADRE Paper   -   three months
- SAASS Thesis   -   three months
- Wright Flyer Paper   -   three months
- Walker Paper   -   three months
- Maxwell Paper   -   six to eight weeks

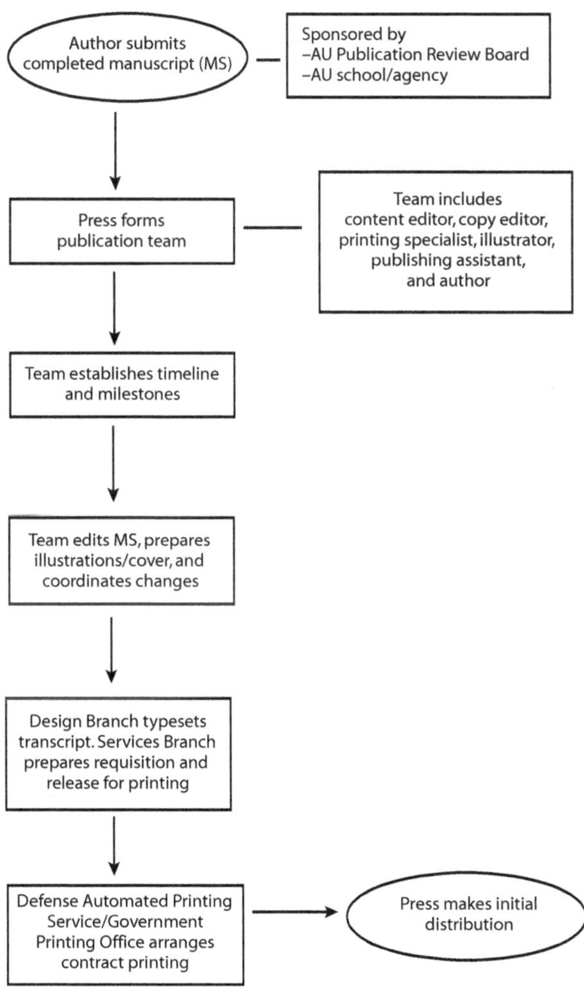

Figure 1. General work flow

Our Authors

AU Press seeks manuscripts from both military and civilian writers on such topics as

- airpower and space power doctrine and strategy,
- the nature and future of airpower's role in warfare and peace,
- the history of airpower and space power,
- case studies of the employment of airpower and space power at all levels of conflict,
- aircraft and weapons systems,
- space applications, and
- biographies of airpower and space power personalities, pioneers, theorists, leaders, and commanders.

Our typical authors include students whose PME school selects his or her paper for publication as part of the series sponsored by that school (e.g., Lt Col Todd G. Kemper, USMC, *Aviation Urban Operations: Are We Training Like We Fight?* Maxwell Paper no. 33 [2004]). We also publish books written by students or staff members, designed for use by multiple Air Force agencies—whether in PME curricula or major-command training programs—and designated AU-numbered texts (e.g., Maj David Beens et al., AU-2, *Guidelines for Command: A Handbook on the Leadership of People for Air Force Commanders and Supervisors* [2003]). Furthermore, individuals who submit a manuscript to the AU Publication Review Board can obtain approval to have it published by AU Press (e.g., Capt Matthew K. Rodman, *A War of Their Own: Bombs over the Southwest Pacific* [2005]). The press also publishes special studies at the behest of higher headquarters, such as *Air Force 2025* (1996).

As a prospective author, you should find the information contained in this guide useful as you go about assembling and submitting your manuscript to us for publication. If you have no sponsor at Air University and wish to have your study considered by the Publication Review Board, please send a printed copy of the manuscript, along with a cover letter that identifies your probable audience, describes your project's value to the Air Force, and tells us about your background and expertise, to the Deputy Director, Air University Press, AUL/LP, 131 West Shumacher Avenue, Maxwell AFB, Alabama 36112-6615. If we accept your manuscript for publication, we will send you a publishing agreement (see appendix A) to read, sign, and return to us. This document specifies, among other things, the obligations of both you and the Air Force as they pertain to the publication of your work.

Submitting Material

After we have accepted your study for publication and you have signed and returned the publishing agreement, we ask that you assemble your manuscript for final submission. Specifically, we require a printed, properly formatted copy of the entire manuscript; electronic files of the manuscript on disk or CD; all necessary permissions; properly formatted illustrations (electronic files of illustrations should be on a separate disk or CD); signatures and date of birth; and a distribution list. If you have questions, stylistic or otherwise, as you prepare your manuscript, please contact us; consult part one of this publication, *Air University Style Guide for Writers and Editors*; or refer to *The Chicago Manual of Style* (15th edition).

Formatting Your Manuscript

- Submit one unbound, single-sided or double-sided, double-spaced copy of the complete manuscript on 8.5" x 11" paper in 12-point font (we prefer Bookman Old Style). Front matter, notes, and back matter should be double spaced as well.
- Number the pages consecutively throughout, from the first page of the front matter to the last page of the back matter.
- Place notes at the end of each chapter. They should be double spaced and in the same size font as the rest of the manuscript.
- Make sure that your hierarchy of subheadings is consistent (see *AU Style Guide*, 1.53). Do not use numbered subheadings.
- Check all quotations against the original sources and extract needed documentation for endnotes and bibliography as required.
- Provide translations or paraphrases of passages in foreign languages in parentheses following the passage or in brackets if the passage is a block quotation.
- Number your illustrations and tables consecutively throughout the manuscript (e.g., Figure 1, Figure 2, etc.; Table 1, Table 2, etc.). Indicate the placement of each illustration or table by including its number and caption in the text (e.g., following the paragraph in which you refer to the illustration or table). Include a credit line, if applicable. Insert a copy of the illustration or table on the page following that citation (include the number of the illustration or table on the copy). For example,

Figure 9. Cutaway view of the B-25G. (Reprinted from North American Aviation, "Train Dispatcher," *Saturday Evening Post*, 4 November 1944, 107.)

Table 2. Bomb strikes during the Battle of the Bismarck Sea

[credit line, placed below table] *Reprinted from* Air Evaluation Board, Southwest Pacific Area, "Battle of the Bismarck Sea and Development of Masthead Attacks," 1 July 1945, 47, Air Force Historical Research Agency, Maxwell AFB, AL.

• Include a list of illustrations and list of tables as part of the table of contents.

• If possible, submit an alphabetized list of key terms that we can use to prepare an index.

Assemble your manuscript in the following order:

• title page
• dedication (optional)
• table of contents (except Wright Flyer Papers and Maxwell Papers)
• foreword (optional; required for Walker Papers)
• about the author (except Wright Flyer Papers)
• abstract (required for Walker Papers)
• preface (optional for Walker Papers)
• acknowledgments (optional)
• introduction (optional)
• text
• appendixes (optional)
• glossary/list of abbreviations (optional but strongly encouraged in manuscripts that make extensive use of abbreviations/acronyms)
• bibliography (except SAAS theses and Maxwell Papers)
• list of key terms for index (books; sometimes Fairchild Papers and CADRE Papers)

Electronic Files

• Along with your printed copy, submit electronic files of your manuscript on floppy disk, zip disk, or CD in a format compatible with Microsoft Windows (e.g., Word, WordPerfect). The electronic files should match the printout exactly.

• Label each disk with your name, title of your work, the contents of the disk, and the level of classification, if applicable.

• Do not use special fonts or combinations of fonts and type sizes, special color coding or spacing, templates, embedded styles for the table of contents or index, or similar desktop-publishing features.

• Create a separate file for each part of the front matter (e.g., contents, foreword, preface, etc.), each chapter, and each part of the back matter (e.g., appendixes, glossary/list of abbreviations, bibliography, etc.).

• Do not embed illustrations or tables in the text files. Instead, include them as separate electronic files (see also "Formatting Your Illustrations," below). Embedded endnotes are encouraged.

• Do not use your word processor's automatic bulleting/numbering feature.

Permissions

• According to the terms of your publishing agreement with us, you guarantee that your work is original. Therefore, if you do use copyrighted written, graphic, or pictorial material, you must obtain written permissions from the rights holders and submit copies to us, along with instructions from the rights holders concerning credit lines and publication limitations. You are also responsible for the payment of any necessary fees to the rights holders. After we begin editing your manuscript, if we think you need to obtain additional permissions, we will contact you as soon as possible.

• You do not need to obtain permission if the material you use is in the public domain or if you comply with the doctrine of fair use. For further information on such material, see part one of this publication, *Air University Style Guide for Writers and Editors*, appendix C.

• In the case of material developed for school coursework, the OPR in the using organization is responsible for reviewing permissions and ensuring that the use of the copyrighted material adheres to any limitations or requests indicated by the rights holder (see Air Force Instruction [AFI] 33-360, vol. 1, *Air Force Content Management Program—Publications*, 30 January 2004; and AFI 51-303, *Intellectual Property—Patents, Patent-Related Matters, Trademarks and Copyrights*, 1 September 1998).

• Provide AU Press with copies of permissions and, if applicable, AF Form 9, Request for Purchase, along with DD Form 1155, Order for Supplies or Services.

• Because obtaining permissions can take a long time, begin requesting them early in the process of preparing your manuscript.

Formatting Your Illustrations

• Submit original, hard-copy illustrations such as photos, maps, or figures (line drawings). Please send us a current photo of you for inclusion in the "About the Author" section and for placement on the back cover of your book. More than one pose is permissible. The photo for "About the Author" should be black and white; the one for the back cover can be color. We will return all original illustrations to you after we have processed them.

• If you scan your own images, please do so in accordance with our resolution requirements (see appendix B) and submit them as separate electronic files. We discourage the use of PowerPoint files.

• Our artists design and create attractive covers for our publications. Although we reserve the right to make final artistic decisions about the cover of your book, if you have ideas about artwork, our illustrators will be happy to work with you to bring them to fruition. Please send us your notes and/or sketches and contact the chief of our Design Branch at 334-953-2774 or DSN 493-2774.

Signatures and Date of Birth

• Provide your signature as well as that of the person who writes your foreword (if included) in black ink, each on a separate sheet of white bond paper. Our printing specialists will transfer them to the signature blocks at the end of the preface and foreword of your manuscript.

• Provide us your birth year; the Library of Congress includes it as part of the cataloging-in-publication (CIP) information for your book.

Distribution List

• You may submit a list of names and addresses of people to whom we will send a copy of your book. We will provide you up to 50 copies of your book free of charge—25 for you and 25 for the individuals on your list. We will make additional copies available on a case-by-case basis.

Please send all materials, including a filled-out copy of the author's checklist (appendix C) to the

Deputy Director
Air University Press, AUL/LP
131 West Shumacher Avenue
Maxwell AFB, Alabama 36112-6615

APPENDIX A

Publishing Agreement

Publishing Agreement

This is a formal agreement between the United States Air Force (termed "**Air Force**" hereafter) and ____ (termed the "**Writer**" hereafter) to publish _____ [publication type] (termed the "**Work**" hereafter) and titled _____. The Writer agrees to abide by the terms and conditions set forth below. The agreement is effective as of _____.

1. Engagement and Relationships: The Air Force agrees to publish, and the Writer licenses the Air Force to publish, the Work under the terms and conditions set forth in this agreement.

2. Compensation: The Writer will receive no monetary compensation of any kind from the Air Force.

3. License: In exchange for publication and distribution of the Work at no cost to the Writer, the Writer grants the Air Force a permanent, nonexclusive, nontransferable, royalty-free license to publish and distribute the Work, in whole or in part, to Department of Defense (DOD) personnel, both military and civilian, in whatever quantities and at whatever times the Air Force determines is necessary for the education of DOD personnel. The Air Force agrees that it shall not distribute the Work to any person not affiliated with the DOD.

4. Retention of Copyright: Nothing in this agreement shall be interpreted to transfer the Writer's ownership of the Work to the Air Force. The Writer shall retain all rights to the Work not transferred to the Air Force under this agreement. The Air Force agrees to include language in any volume or other media containing the Work stating that the Writer retains ownership of the Work and all rights granted under 17 U.S.C. §106, except those rights which have been granted to the Air Force under this agreement.

5. Format: The Air Force may, without limitation, publish the Work in hard copy and in electronic or any other media format and in any language.

6. Publication Costs: The Air Force will pay full costs for the publication of the Work for distribution to Air Force personnel, including the initial run of the Work and any reprints or additional runs the Air Force, in its sole discretion, elects to produce.

7. Development of the Work: The Air Force reserves the right to edit or otherwise modify the Work as the Air Force deems appropriate. As part of its normal preparation for publication, the Air Force will typically (1) perform substantive and copy edits of the manuscript along with other quality-control measures to conform to Air University (AU) Press standards and style; (2) design front and back covers; (3) create or further develop graphics to support the narrative content of the Work; (4) schedule reprints of the Work; and (5) distribute the Work to addresses on its standard distributions list. Check all of the following that apply:

☐ The Air Force will perform a substantive edit of the Work.

☐ The Air Force will perform a copy edit of the Work.

☐ The Air Force will design a cover for the Work.

☐ The Air Force will create graphics for the Work.

☐ The Air Force will prepare the Work for printing; complete a DD Form 282, Printing Requisition/Order; and then return the prepress package to the Writer.

☐ The Air Force will not distribute the Work.

8. Obligations: The Writer agrees to coordinate with the Air Force by responding promptly to inquiries or requests for materials within 10 working days after the Air Force makes a request but no longer than 20 working days unless extenuating circumstances, deployment, or other unforeseeable circumstances warrant an extension to 30 working days. The Air Force will have no obligation to publish the Work when the Writer does not respond to inquiries or requests within 90 working days or when DOD, Air Education and Training Command, Air Force, or AU policy or command decisions preclude publication.

9. Delivery and Acceptance of the Work: The Writer agrees to deliver to the Air University Press the complete and final manuscript for the Work no later than ______. The Writer shall deliver the original Work inclusive of illustrations, charts, graphs, and any other material satisfactorily to the Air University Press in a double-spaced hard copy, along with a diskette/CD in Microsoft Word, and in accordance with guidelines in the *Air University Style and Author Guide*. If the Writer fails to deliver a complete or satisfactory manuscript by the date above, the Air Force will have the right, at its discretion, to extend the date of publication or to terminate this agreement. For reprint editions of previously published works by other publishers, the Writer (or Editor) may deliver or the Air Force will obtain the latest printing of a publication from which to produce the reprint edition. The Air Force will also address and secure any copyright releases required from previous publishers to allow reprinting of the Work by the Air Force.

10. Writer Affirmations: The Writer affirms that the Work will be original, will not infringe upon any copyright protections, and will not contain plagiarized text or graphics, specifically as indicated by checking each of the following statements:

☐ The content of the Work is accurate, based on sound research practices, and constitutes a complete manuscript with all front matter, narrative text, graphics, and back matter included at submission—with the exception of an index, which the Air Force will create in the final production stage and for which the author may be requested to provide a seed list.

☐ Should the Air Force determine during preliminary review or after acceptance for publication that the Work contains material of which the Writer is not the writer or proprietor, the Writer agrees to obtain permission to reproduce such material at no expense to the Air Force and to provide copies of the permission(s) to the Air Force within the time periods specified in paragraph 8 above.

☐ The Work contains no recipe, formula, or instruction that if applied could cause readers personal harm or injury.

☐ The Work in no way infringes on the right of privacy of any person or entity, including organizations, institutions, copyright holders, or others, as a result of plagiarism, libel, slander, or any other misuse of material included in the original Work.

☐ The Work does not contain profane language or quotations containing profane language.

☐ The Work contains no classified or restricted information.

11. Academic Freedom: The Air Force encourages and defends the rights of both students and faculty in accordance with Air University Instruction (AUI) 36-2308, *Academic Freedom*. The Air Force advocates the right of the Writer to exercise full freedom of literary investigation and expression. Only the adherence to security classification limits the Writer's freedom to expound upon subject matter of the Work, as long as the Writer maintains accuracy and respects the proprietary rights of others. Further, the Air Force endorses all established practices of academic freedom as stated in the *AU Faculty Handbook* and AUI 36-2308. The Air Force will not publish profanity but will revise or otherwise rework the narrative to indicate the use of expletives in quotations. Air University Public Affairs is the security and policy review authority for all information and material concerning military matters available for release.

12. Writer's Name and Likeness: The Writer agrees that the Air Force shall have the right to use the Writer's name, likeness, and biographical materials concerning him/her in the original Work, in revised or derivative editions, or in Air Force advertisements or promotional materials.

13. Writer's Copies: Upon publication of the first printing of the Work, the Air Force shall provide the Writer—without cost—up to 50 copies of the Work. The Air Force will send the Writer up to 25 personal copies of the Work at an address the Writer specifies to the distribution clerk and up to 25 copies to addressees on a mailing list the Writer provides to the Air Force. Additional copies will be provided on a case-by-case basis at the deputy's or director's discretion.

Entire Agreement: This document constitutes the Agreement between the parties and supersedes any other promises, conditions, understandings, or terms, whether oral or written. Any addenda to this Agreement must be modified in writing and signed by the Writer (or a representative of the Writer) and parties at the Air Force.

For the Air Force by

___________________________   ___________________________

Writer's Signature (Date)   Chief, Editorial Branch (Date)

                                      Air University Press

                                      ____

                                      Deputy Director (Date)

                                      Air University Press

                                      ____

                                      Director (Date)

                                      Air University Press

Definitions of Terms

Back Matter—Elements following the main text of a book. In order, they include appendix(es), chronology (if not in front matter), abbreviations (if not in front matter), glossary, bibliography, list of contributors, and index(es).

Copy Edit—A process concerned with the mechanics of written communication. It refers to consistency in capitalization, spelling, hyphenation, numbers, documentation, formatting of the document in accordance with the press's house standards, and so forth. It also encompasses attention to grammar, syntax, and basic usage.

Cover Design—The process of preparing illustrative material or decorative patterns for reproduction on the outer binding of a book, accomplished by Air University Press illustrators in consultation with the book's author.

Create—To bring into existence something new by means of imaginative skill or other action, as in the production of original graphics or textual material (e.g., an index).

Distribution List—A roster of names and addresses of individuals and institutions to whom Air University Press sends it publications. The term refers to both the press's standard list of recipients as well as a custom list provided by the author.

Front Matter—Elements preceding the main text of a book. In order, they include the title page, copyright page, dedication, epigraph, table of contents, list of illustrations, list of tables, foreword, about the author [Air University Press publications], preface, acknowledgments (if not part of preface), introduction (if not part of text), abbreviations (if not part of back matter), and chronology (if not in back matter).

Graphics—Products of pictorial art, such as paintings, drawings, and so forth, used especially for illustrating or decorating printed matter.

Narrative—The written representation of an event, a story, or an account.

Plagiarism—Entails appropriating the literary composition of other people, parts or passages of their writings, or the ideas or language of the same, and using them as one's own. Copying verbatim without quotation marks with the intent to claim that material as one's own constitutes plagiarism, as does the intentional use, without credit, of a source's sentence structure and style with only minor changes.

Prepare/Develop—To make ready for use, put together in a certain form, create, or produce, especially as related to the preparation/development of a publication.

Substantive Edit—A process concerned with the organization and presentation of content. It includes rephrasing to eliminate ambiguity, reorganizing or tightening, simplifying, recasting, and so forth.

APPENDIX B

Submitting Images for Publication

Please submit original images such as photos, maps, or figures (line drawings). We will return them to you. Note that .gif and .jpg files are not normally acceptable for printing due to their low resolution. If any problems arise as you prepare images for submission, please contact us.

If you wish to scan your own images, please keep the following principles in mind. In order that the file contain enough data to reproduce accurately, you should use high-end black-and-white/color calibrated scanning equipment. Scan all images (color and grayscale) at a resolution between 266 and 300 pixels per inch, based on an input-to-output (I/O) size ratio of one to one. For example, a three-by-five-inch original photograph to be printed at three-by-five inches (I/O ratio of one to one) should be scanned at 266 to 300 pixels per inch. The same size photo to be printed at six-by-ten inches (I/O ratio of one to two) should be scanned at 532 to 600 pixels per inch. All other enlargements and reductions are similarly proportional. Save your images either as uncompressed TIFF (tagged image file format), native PhotoShop file format (.psd), or EPS (encapsulated postscript) files.

Do not import images into another document such as Microsoft Word for submission. Submit images as individual files only. You may create a directory or folder with subdirectories to organize your images.

Please note that images scanned at lower resolutions and then forced or pushed to a higher resolution to meet printing standards become blurry. This happens, for example, if you change an image at 150 pixels per inch to 300 pixels per inch in your image-editing program. Instead, you should rescan the image at the target resolution of 300 pixels per inch. Although you can reduce digital images to a desired resolution, you should never try to increase them to a higher resolution to meet printing standards.

Scan all line art as bitmap images with a resolution of between 1,200 and 2,540 pixels per inch, based on an I/O ratio of one to one. Enlargements and reductions are similarly proportional. Save the images either as uncompressed TIFF, native PhotoShop file format, or EPS files.

If you have any questions or need assistance, please call Air University Press's Design Branch at 334-953-2774 or DSN 493-2774.

APPENDIX C

Author's Checklist

Air University Press
Author's Checklist

Title ____

Author ____

Date ____

Text (use either a check mark or an "NA" [not applicable] for each item, as appropriate)

___One printed copy of the manuscript.

___Manuscript pages numbered consecutively and double-spaced throughout.

___Notes double-spaced and grouped at the end of each chapter.

___Text reflects placement of illustrations and tables.

___My signature for preface.

___Signature of person who wrote foreword.

___My date of birth for CIP data.

___List of key terms for index.

___Properly labeled disk(s) or CD(s) that exactly match the hard copy of the manuscript.

___Copyright permissions for textual passages, illustrations, tables, photos, and other graphics; sources properly acknowledged in manuscript.

___My distribution list.

Illustrations (use either a check mark or an "NA" [not applicable] for each item, as appropriate)

___Original prints, transparencies, and/or camera-ready copies of illustrations, graphs, maps, and so forth. Copy of each illustration placed after page on which it is to appear in printed manuscript.

___Properly labeled disk of illustrations (separate from the manuscript disk).

___Permissions for illustrations; sources properly acknowledged in manuscript.

___Double-spaced caption list of illustrations and tables included in table of contents.

AU-1

Air University Style and Author Guide

Air University Press Team

Chief Editor
Marvin Bassett

Copy Editor
Sherry Terrell

Book Design and Cover Art
L. Susan Fair

*Composition and
Prepress Production*
Vivian D. O'Neal

Print Preparation
Joan Hickey

Distribution
Diane Clark

9 781780 399744